ABOUT THE AUTHOR . . .

P9-BZV-794

JAMES H. JAUNCEY, the eldest of fifteen children, was reared in the Australian wilderness in a home of poverty and privation. Despite these
handicaps, Dr. Jauncey holds ten academic degrees, earned from universities in Perth, Australia; Melbourne,
Australia; London, England; Berke-
ley, California and others, and has a
background of experience in science,
engineering, psychology, education,
religion and journalism. In 1948 he
came to America, becoming a natural-
ized citizen in 1954. Presently minister of the First Christian Church, El
Paso, Texas, he is well known as an
author and lecturer and is listed in
Who's Who in American Education.

Above Ourselves

BY THE SAME AUTHOR . . .

Science Returns to God
I Believe in the American Way
This Faith We Live By
This Power Within

Above Ourselves

THE ART OF TRUE HAPPINESS

by

JAMES H. JAUNCEY

ZONDERVAN PUBLISHING HOUSE
GRAND RAPIDS   MICHIGAN

ABOVE OURSELVES
Copyright 1964 by
Zondervan Publishing House
Grand Rapids, Michigan

Library of Congress Catalog Card Number 64-25223

Printed in the United States of America

248.42
J 41

Foreword

This book contains advice on practical methods of achieving human happiness. It is an attempt to show that almost all unhappiness has one basic cause: the failure of the inexorable drive of the personality to find ego fulfillment. Happy, contented living results when this drive is guided into its normal channels. Armed with this one tool, the human engineer can cope with almost any human problem. The author has been using this approach successfully for many years.

The great unifying force of man's nature is personality drive, the hunger to achieve. This is what the Bible is referring to when its talks about pride and humility. You can diagnose almost everything about human nature by this one principle: when a person is achieving the maximum of which his personality is capable, he is happy; when he is frustrated in this goal, he is unhappy.

22155

Contents

War on Human Unhappiness

1

War on Human Unhappiness

From the time man first set foot on earth, God has been waging a war against human unhappiness. At the very beginning of history He set the standard for living right. It was found in the peaceful, joyous experience of the Garden of Eden. When Paradise was lost, it was on man's initiative, not God's.

The *circumstances* of Eden can never again be repeated on this earth — the ramifications of evil are too deep-seated for that. But the possibility of attaining to the *heart* of Eden is still possible. The Bible insists that happy, vibrant, purposeful living is within the reach of every man, and that this inner treasure is inviolate against the inroads of unpleasant circumstances.

According to the Bible, God does not just passively wait for us to discover abundant living. He is desperately searching for us, battling against the evils that would destroy us, eager to lift us above ourselves and give us happiness.

The Old Testament repeatedly tells of the prosperity and joy of those who will follow God's way. This message was driven home by the burning words of the prophets and the even more harrowing lessons of bitter experience. But the divine crusade to restore unhappy man to Eden did not stop at this. In a last

11

desperate effort, God sent His Son, who openly proclaimed that He had come to bring abundant life. Since then His Spirit has been working in and through the hearts of men to give them the vision of the Promised Land and help them attain it.

Here is a drastically different outlook from that of most modern writing, especially fiction, where man is depicted as a helpless, suffering, tortured and often degraded creature, drowning in his own filth. It is merely the shadow world of minds and hearts in prison. The real world does have its clouds and its darkness, but it is still a world of sunshine, of light, of color, of beauty, of happiness. This real world is reached through a man's innermost soul.

The Bible is clear in naming sin as the cause of human unhappiness. However, by "sin" it does not so much mean individual acts of wrongdoing, as rebellion against God's plan for man's life. The sin of pride is seen as the root of the trouble, for pride is primarily rebellion. On the other hand, humility is praised as the secret of human well-being.

Pride is the personality drive out of control, blindly seeking satisfaction regardless of God or others. Humility is the will and the ego under control, poised, finding satisfaction in the ways God intended.

The secret of happiness therefore lies in carrying out those plans for the personality which God Himself has made. The human personality is so constructed that this is the only way it can function properly. These plans are not only found in the Bible, but also within us, like a plate with instructions that the maker has placed on a machine.

As an engineer, I found great satisfaction in working on a piece of equipment and then seeing it begin to run smoothly and efficiently. However, I get an infinitely greater satisfaction when I go to work on the human machine and help to restore it to the proper working order which the Great Designer intended.

When a malfunction occurs in a machine, the engineer attacks the problem with the pre-supposition that this is abnormal, therefore, the proper operation can be restored. He doesn't attribute the trouble to fate, cussedness, the weather or the economic system.

In the human machine, we call the malfunction "unhappiness." When functioning properly, we experience a pleasant emotional glow — "happiness." This was the way God intended things to be. The Creation account in the Bible affirms that God made sure everything was "good." Happy, contented living, then, is the norm. Although unhappiness is widespread, it is, nevertheless, the abnormal.

When human unhappiness occurs, it is no more due to fate, cussedness, the weather or the economic system than is the malfunction of any other machine. In other words, the possibility of restoration is under our control with one vital exception, and that is the interference of the human will, something a machine does not have.

When a machine breaks down, usually the owner stands helplessly by. He may remove the cover, peer into it and maybe say a few appropriate words, but in the end he has to call a mechanic. The owner may be more highly educated and even more intelligent than the mechanic, but the mechanic knows the laws of the machine, and that's what counts. It doesn't take him long to locate the cause of the trouble and from then on the repair is routine.

Although people are far more complicated than machines, we are governed largely by laws, indeed by one great principle. When we recognize this law we can, as human engineers, trace the trouble, and with skill and patience bring about happy living again.

When I went to school, psychology, the study of human

behavior, was in its early stages. The human being was supposed to be composed of a host of instinctive drives. As a matter of fact, it seemed to me that all one had to do to get an M.A. or Ph.D. was to discover some instinct that no one had thought of before and write a thesis on it.

This made a nightmare of counseling. To be scientific one had to examine each of these drives, find out which had gone wrong, and then set it straight. Unfortunately many of them hadn't been discovered, so there were two strikes against you before you started. Now we know that a personality is much more than an aggregate of instincts. A person is a unity and must be studied and treated as such.

Medical Science provides a good illustration of this new attitude. A doctor no longer merely treats symptoms. He treats the whole person. Symptoms are used merely as a guide to his diagnosis in determining what is wrong with the body as a whole. When the cure is effected, the symptoms disappear.

During the course of my own counseling experience, it has been necessary to cope with a wide variety of problems: mental depression, boredom, psychophysical symptoms, crime, delinquency, marriage disorders, personality maladjustments, failure to succeed, religious unhappiness and so on. In the vast majority of cases the primary cause of the trouble originates with the *personality operating at a level far below its potential.* If the unhappy person can be helped to find a challenging and satisfying way of life, the symptoms begin to disappear like fog before the sunshine.

Now, there are disorders which may become so chronic that psychiatric help is indicated — possibly even shock treatment; but fortunately this is not the case with most of us. Even in the case of the psychotic, with all the psychiatric care in the world, happiness cannot be realized until he finds the satisfying life of full achievement. This drive of the personality to emerge, achieve and find recognition, is with us from the cradle to the grave.

Take an infant who is a few weeks old, hold his hands and feet so that he cannot move, and he immediately bellows out his anger and distress. At this early stage, physical movement is the only way he has of personality expression. When this is inhibited, he experiences the first taste of an anguish that comes from personality frustration.

Part of the responsibility of being a parent consists in preventing young children from undertaking potentially dangerous adventures even though these prohibitions may occasionally produce an explosion. The child is being blindly impelled by forces within him to venture, and when he is stopped, even for the best reasons in the world, his unhappiness is obvious and vocal.

This is the teenage dilemma. Adolescence is a no man's land. It is difficult to know exactly where a parent's authority ends and the child's begins. Meanwhile, emerging adulthood is forcing young people to find a place in the sun as independent beings. In this process they are hindered by their own personality limitations, by their physical powers, by their economic resources, by competition with others, by their parents, by the law and dozens of other factors. To the extent that they succeed in expressing themselves, they are happy. But should they fail, the misery is intense. Is it any wonder that suicide is a major cause of death among teenagers? Is the apparent irrationality of juvenile delinquency so hard to understand?

Marriage is ruled by the same law. As a matter of fact, two persons may love each other desperately but still be unsuited to live with each other. In the romantic desire for oneness it is easy to forget that the individual personality needs must also be satisfied. Unless each is finding achievement apart from the other, the repressed personality power will blast the marriage wide open. Divorce is seldom caused by the faults that hit the headlines. These are merely symptoms. One, or both, of the personality machines had ground to a halt long before. Frequently the frailties seen in the other person are merely the projection of one's own unhappy heart.

Then again, a person's job or profession offers far more than merely the means of earning a living. It is an opportunity for self-realization and recognition. The pay increase or the promotion means much more than money. These are symbols of success in achievement, rewarding to the ego. On the other hand, demotion, dismissal, lack of recognition may drive a man to suicide, drink, immorality, to degradation and Skid Row.

Probably the ego drive is most devastating in old age when normally there are no longer the physical powers nor the opportunities to find satisfying expression. The anguish that older people often experience is heartrending. When the elderly man repeats the same story over and over again, he may know he is boring you, but he can't help himself. Talk is the only means he has for self-expression now. Satisfaction is the dim glow found in reliving exploits long since past.

The happiness that comes from self-realization is independent of material circumstances. Money and leisure may make life more pleasant for a person, but they do not necessarily produce happiness. Many wealthy people are desperately unhappy and many poor people are supremely content. Actually, wealth can cut off the possibility of happiness by killing the opportunity to achieve. If we can buy anything we want, there is little place for that invigorating struggle against odds to achieve our goals.

A man is not like a dog. Fill a dog's stomach, give him a comfortable place on which to lie, and he is content. People require much more. The body enjoys the comfort of inactivity and sloth, but the spirit allows no peace except through the pursuit of self-realization.

The pilgrimage to abundant living never ends. Once a goal

is achieved, it must be replaced by another even more difficult, even more inaccessible, even more challenging.

We are human engineers to the extent in which we can find our own way into this abundant life — or in which we can guide others into that way.

At this point you may wonder why this whole matter of happiness and personal achievement is so complicated and involved. Why can't we just pray to God, the Designer, and let Him take care of everything? God could do this if He wished, but the truth is that He prefers to work through human means. For example, God could quite easily place our food ready-cooked on our tables, but He doesn't. Instead, He makes us go through the human process of tilling, planting, tending, reaping, processing, distributing, purchasing, preparing and cooking.

If God intended to act solely in a supernatural way, much of the New Testament would be completely unnecessary. Instead He has given us the most detailed instructions for spiritual and physical well being. In applying these to ourselves and others, we are engineers working on the human machine.

This does not mean that prayer is unnecessary: far from it! Our instructions call for it. Through prayer, God gives skill and guidance so that we can restore the sense of well-being and abundant living He wants us to enjoy.

Religion for Living

2

Religion for Living

Man is incurably religious. As far back as we know, he has always been the same. Even now, no matter how primitive the tribe, religion for good or ill is an overshadowing reality that permeates, and often determines his everyday living.

Religious experience satisfies, because, in it, the personality becomes identified with a Power beyond itself. As we have seen, the prime law governing human beings is the drive of the personality to grow and achieve. The more we do this, the more we find ourselves in the society of those who have received recognition for their achievements. Acquaintance with the successful gives a peculiar sense of satisfaction because it is the symbol of our own progress. Through religion we can cultivate a conscious relationship with the ultimate in greatness, God Himself.

The communists have worked at getting rid of religion in their society, but have been unsuccessful. Even now in Russia, after nearly a half century of anti-religious propaganda complete with economic, social and even physical "persuasion," the religious tide is high. Half of all Russian children are baptized at birth, surreptitious though this act may be.

Irreligion has become a religion with the communists. As a matter of fact, we could wish Christians were as devoted to Christ as communists are to their cause! Communists even imitate religious observances, with their "confession of sins" against the party and their veneration of "saints" such as Lenin and Marx. In China they even have a counterpart of Christian Endeavor for young people.

Seeking to stem the religious urge in man is as hopeless as King Canute ordering back the ocean tide. This does not mean that the religious drive is always satisfied even if we follow through with it. Today there are 114,000,000 church members in America, yet many of these have not found the secret of happy living. In fact, we sometimes find as many or more problems in the church as outside. Needy, unhappy people are often drawn to the church in desperation and their presence often produces dissension and bickering. Many try religion and abandon it, because they have become disappointed or even bitter.

A religious faith can only continue to satisfy if it becomes a fulfillment of the fundamental drive of human beings for personality achievement.

On the other hand, superficial involvement in religion can neither satisfy man's inner desire for faith nor his need for fulfillment through faith. The carrying out of religious observances, with the hope that God will reward with inner peace and contentment, is useless. God does not work that way. He works *through us*.

Many people prefer to be on the fringe of religion without becoming "involved." They identify themselves with the Church either by membership, attendance at services or by giving general approval to its mission, but are unwilling to become involved in its activities. Their role is that of the silent partner in a firm, a part of it, but taking no action in its affairs. This attitude pays no dividends in terms of abundant living.

Even a real conversion in which God enters the heart is no guarantee of permanent happiness. It is true that conversion is often accompanied by a tremendous surge of religious emotion, but this frequently abates with time. The convert may be a child of God, but he can also be unhappy and miserable.

The joy that can come through religious experience is not a separate emotion. The capacity for happiness is innate in the personality; it only needs to be released. But this can only be experienced when the inner potential is finding its full realization. Vital religious experience draws this out and brings with it the inevitable emotional glow which is the mark of true self-realization. If religion fails to do this, even though it is of divine origin, it is powerless to help.

Christianity is a way of living and gives its rewards only to those who live out its implications. It makes tremendous demands upon the personality, but offers the highest satisfaction in return.

If we want the best that God intends for us, our commitment to Him must be total. This is faith — a faith that goes far beyond mere *belief*. It means having such confidence in Christ that the whole life is committed to Him to be lived *His way* regardless of the cost. The outward expression of this involvement will differ from person to person, but it does entail following through with whatever He says to the heart.

This does not demand a withdrawal from life: far from it. We are called on to enjoy life materially and spiritually. It is the way we live it that makes the difference: the purpose behind the living. Living for its own sake is meaningless and empty. Living for God and others, with a sense of divine mission, gives zest and purpose to it all.

Total commitment does not cause us to become unbalanced. Instead, the reverse is true. The fanatic is not totally committed in his heart, so he compensates for this by a whitewash job. He is paying for his guilt by surface religious activity. Total commitment puts an end to inner conflict and therefore is the only way to peace. When the war inside stops, we can see the whole of life with a true perspective.

If a doctor discovered an operable cancer mass in the body, the patient wouldn't settle for less than total action. Certainly no one would be foolish enough to say to his doctor: "Let's not go overboard, doctor. Don't take the whole thing out. Just remove part, and then we'll work up toward getting the rest out later."

If we mean business about finding the good life, it must be unconditional surrender. No rationalizing. No restrictions. We may not have the power to break loose from everything we know to be wrong, but we have to be *willing* to let go. Then God will do the rest.

Total commitment means enthusiastically and unreservedly giving ourselves to God to help Him accomplish His mission of redemption. His work becomes ours.

I know a young schoolteacher who joined the church after coming to the conclusion that her mixed-up life was caused by spiritual inadequacy. She expected a miracle to happen, but she wasn't willing to pay the price.

"I'm joining the church," she said, "but I don't want to be tied down. I won't promise to come to church every Sunday. Sometimes I stay out rather late on Saturday nights and I like to sleep in. And I don't want to go to Sunday school. I had a enough of that when I was a kid. Choir? No, I don't think so. Maybe if the practice were not on Thursdays. I have a T.V. program that I like to watch that night."

She's out of the church now! She claims that she tried religion and it didn't do anything for her. She didn't even give God a chance.

Total commitment does not mean giving *all* our time, talent and money to the church, but it does mean taking up our share of the load.

Let's face it. Even in our more or less Christian society such commitment involves personal loss, sacrifice and self-denial. We can't have Christianity without a cross. But it's worth it.

We have something to live for. When the personality is totally extended God-ward, the streams of inner joy begin to flow.

Perhaps you have a mental block toward taking such a step. You are not an atheist, but neither are you sure about God, and you are even less sure about Christian doctrine and the Bible. Possibly you are making an intellectual approach. The Apostle Paul, himself an intellectual giant, warns that God cannot be reached that way.

We don't fall in love intellectually, nor can we prove that a sunset is lovely or a symphony is beautiful. But we know these things nevertheless. The mind can only take us a certain distance. It can show that the existence of God is reasonable, but we must always take that step of faith. Once that is done, intellectual proof becomes as meaningless as attempting to prove the fact of existence.

In a way faith is a bit like learning to swim. Theorizing about it on the bank of the river is not enough; you have to get into the water. Even when the plunge is taken, certainty does not always come at once. It grows with the adventure, providing the commitment is total.

Personal commitment actually involves much more than mere *identification* with religion. It is possible to be members of a church for many years and yet be strangers to God. The presence of God has to be practiced. We *develop* an acquaintance with God by prayer, meditation and living His kind of life. As faith is rewarded by a felt awareness of God, life receives one of its deepest satisfactions. We are on terms of personal acquaintance with the Creator of the universe.

This aspect of religious satisfaction is much more than mere snob appeal, like being acquainted with royalty. The New Testament teaches that we have become of royal blood. In the moment of conversion the Spirit of God has entered the heart and made us one with God. His Spirit is flowing through our spiritual veins. God is within us and we are in God. Jesus taught this in the parable of the Vine and the Branches (John 15).

When this relationship is more than a fact of faith and becomes an awareness of experience, the human desire for greatness finds its greatest fulfillment.

Vital religion ministers to the enjoyment of living because it makes what we do important. Leslie Weatherhead once told of what must have been the ultimate in vocational frustration: a woman who made her living making wooden seeds for imitation strawberry jam! Picture a man on an assembly line creating an electronic part and notice how his morale rises when he is told that part is to be used in a space vehicle! His job is now important.

Christianity teaches that the Christian is doing something vitally important. In and through everything he does, material and spiritual, he is cooperating with God as He works unceasingly for the redemption and good of mankind. The New Testament suggests that the Christian is the ambassador for God to the people who do not know Him. When we are consciously allowing God to use us and when we see life in that magnificent perspective, it takes on meaning, significance and purpose.

This requires re-thinking. Instead of our job being *merely* a means of earning a living, God intends that it be a contribution to human welfare. The contribution does not have to be world-shaking — we simply do what God has given us to do and let Him estimate the impact. If our job is making no such contribution, we have no right to be in it.

The Christian view is satisfying to the inner drives of man because it guarantees an *eternal* destiny. Some have criticized the doctrine of immortality as being wishful thinking. It is, but it is not *mere* wishful thinking. Because we long for something does not mean it does not exist. Yearning for human love does not invalidate that emotion. Because we look forward to a salary check does not mean we won't get paid. We do have to make sure that our wishes do not cause us to believe in what we want *on that basis alone.*

The basis of immortality is in God. We are eternal because of our relationship with Him. Whether we feel immortal or not is beside the point. It would have been a devastating blow to the emerging ego of man to find that all his struggles were meaningless, that he was little better than a thinking animal. Therefore when he knows that he shares the very eternity of God, he takes on dignity. The personality gains man makes on earth are not doomed to be lost. They will be transmitted to the life to come as surely as the life of the caterpillar emerges unscathed into the greater existence of the butterfly.

Not only is a vital religious philosophy of life tailor-made to the deepest needs of the emerging personality; it also provides an answer to the problems raised by those evil things that prevent a man from realizing his dreams. There is no greater misery and shame than that which comes when a person realizes he has become a slave to the destructive habits, turbulent moods, and driving obsessions so much a part of human nature.

Christianity is a practical religion. It is aware that these habits and obsessions can become so entrenched that even the most heroic efforts of the human will are powerless to dislodge them. It advises us not to make a frontal attack, but rather to allow ourselves to be permeated with the Spirit of God within. As that process continues, the evils are progressively driven out. Once again our part in this is not to be merely passive. By prayer, Scripture reading, worship and consciousness of God, we can do much to allow Him to saturate our lives with His Spirit. Then the time will come when we can look ourselves in the face and know we are not slaves but free personalities.

The main thesis of this book is that the personality must be kept under extension. Because of human inertia this is hard to do. Christianity is an enormous help because it demands advance.

In His parable of the Talents, the Lord taught that it was a sin to allow our talent to lie buried. Indeed, His language was much stronger here than that which He used on the occasion of the woman taken in adultery. Her sin was a single act, but undeveloped potential is an unending violation. It robs us of the good life and it impoverishes the community by the enrichment that has been withheld. In the end it affects eternity itself.

This is why Christianity has been so successful in bringing progress and a better life to every country where it has been introduced. Self-realization for God and others has been a prime demand on all converts. Even though the majority of Christians may fail to obey, or may only obey imperfectly, the good released by the few who do is always out of proportion to the number involved.

A professor who was not particularly noted for his overt religiousness, once said that Jesus Christ was the greatest psychologist who ever lived, and the New Testament was the greatest book on psychology ever written. Yes, it is all there, waiting for personal application.

Zest Instead of Insipidity

3

Zest Instead of Insipidity

Monotonous, empty living is abnormal. It is the symptom of malfunction in the human machine, and it can be cured.

As we have seen, the remedy is delightfully simple, although not easy. The happy life comes when the total personality is harnessed to its maximum potential. This does not take much knowledge, but does call for patient skill and a persevering drive.

Our main enemy is human inertia, or if we prefer less euphonious terms, plain laziness. It is the easiest thing in the world to sink into a rut and quietly rot. This is pleasant for the body but brings anguish to the spirit, made as it is in the image of God and destined to soar.

Life was intended to be a happy, fulfilling experience but it often drifts into mere colorless existence or dreary monotony. At times it becomes such an agonizing impossibility that even suicide appears attractive.

Life doesn't start that way. To the child it is an ever-changing, exciting adventure. There is so much to be seen and done that no quiet walk through the days is possible. Each precious moment is captured on the run. The mind is constantly alert, curious, prying, and the body is a twisting, turning, jumping, skipping bundle of concentrated energy. There are no shades of emotion — every feeling is intense and when an emotion has served its purpose, it vanishes without warning to be replaced by what is next in focus.

Of course, childhood is not unalloyed bliss. There are always the tears, the pain, the disappointments, the heartaches. But even in the slums where the child is hungry, cold and neglected, he seems to be able to rise above the sordid. Some of us have seen as much zest in play in a blighted street or abandoned rubbish dump as in a costly modern play center. In a child, life has a habit of shining through even the darkness of evil.

Jesus once made a statement which has proved a mine of spiritual truth ever since: "Except ye be converted and become as little children, ye shall not enter into the kingdom of heaven." The Master is simply saying that anyone who wants to enter this Paradise of God's rule in which abundant and effective living is realized, must again become like little children.

Where do we lose this simple capacity to live joyously? Somewhere along the line, feeling becomes satiated and the energy stills. Then gray monotony takes over. Yet the possibility of recapturing zest in living is always there. We know this is true, because, even without too much conscious effort, zest returns in spots. It is there when we fall in love, when we get married, when we receive a promotion, when we win a coveted award, when recognition comes. It is as though the overcast sky had opened and the sun appeared briefly. But soon it closes again and we are left with the grayness and the drizzle.

What has happened in the transition from childhood to maturity? It isn't that the climate of life has changed; we have merely lost our capacity to soar beyond the clouds.

Have you ever had the experience of boarding a jet in dreary overcast weather and a few moments later flying through it to blue, sunny skies? Beneath us we can still see the clouds but we are in a different world. It takes horsepower to do this, but the plane has plenty and more to spare. Similarly, the human spirit has sufficient power, but it must be pointed toward the skies.

The Book of Proverbs is a fascinating manual on happy, prosperous living. It is significant that this helpful and practical book warns about laziness. It refers to the lazy person as a "sluggard." He is put on the same level as a robber! In a potent passage (13:4) it says: "The soul of the sluggard desireth and hath nothing: but the soul of the diligent shall be made fat." I like the imagery of the fat soul. This is exactly what I am writing about here.

Close behind laziness stands the demon of cowardice. Venturing forward may mean hurt and failure, a bloody-nosed ego. To the fainthearted the wounds take precedence over the thrill of possible victory, so we slink back behind the barricades, resigned to remain slaves of insipidity.

There is actually nothing to fear, for ultimate failure is impossible when we have really tried. Possibly we haven't accomplished the desired goal, but we have ventured. We have achieved reality and that is always a success.

It is a thrill to stand on the spot where history has been made. This is especially true of the land of the Bible. On a couple of occasions I have stood on Mars Hill in Athens where the Apostle Paul poured out his heart to the Greek philosophers. He was alone in Athens and the odds were against him. On his right was the mighty Parthenon on the Acropolis, the symbol of the entrenched might of Greek religion. On his left was the hill where Demosthenes, the greatest orator of all time, had thundered his Philippics without avail. In front, row upon row, sat the cynical sages.

Paul didn't win many converts there, but he tried. He must have gone away disappointed. How was he to know that one day the mighty Parthenon would be in ruins, its religion a bygone curiosity, but Christianity the power over men's minds? That's the secret. Try courageously, and leave the results with God.

No single venture in living satisfies for long. No matter how exciting and absorbing it is at the start, its capacity to satisfy quickly wears off. At first it is a challenge to the personality, but when the conquest is complete, the joy fades. At this point we either have to explore it further or find fresh worlds to conquer.

Human personality is elastic. When we stretch it, we automatically increase its capacity to stretch. The achievement of yesterday satisfied because it put the personality under extension. But that experience cannot satisfy today because it has lost its power to challenge. The inner being has adjusted to the new level, so now only further extension can bring fulfillment.

The intellectual life is a vital part of personality and therefore is subject to the same laws. The capacity of the mind to increase its powers appears to be almost infinite, yet it can also wither and die. While it is growing and under pressure, it brings a sense of well-being. When the tension abates there is uneasiness, frustration and depression.

The whole idea behind education is to keep us headed toward the good life by opening our minds to the wonders of knowledge. But the learning process can become a dreary business; it can become the mere acquisition of intellectual skills to enable us to earn our daily bread. However, if we look upon every new piece of knowledge acquired as a personal conquest, education can become a satisfying adventure.

It is obvious that the intellectual adventure cannot end with graduation from school. All this does is fulfill professional requirements, but the personality need goes on.

Learning should continue in depth and breadth. Unless the intellectual skills learned at school are utilized they quickly rust and become useless. That part of the mind which has been exercised in the particular discipline atrophies. This may be only a tiny part of the total mental picture, but it becomes a center of frustration.

Reading is a vital method of intellectual improvement. Watching television, or listening to the radio, or using the other handy methods of "killing time," is much more effortless, but doesn't offer the rewards available to the serious reader. It is a shocking situation that in this country, many people even with college degrees, do not read as much as one book a week.

Dr. Mortimer Adler has been saying for years that a profound education can be achieved by reading his Great Books series. Many people agree and make a gesture toward this goal by purchasing the set, but then leave the books to adorn a bookshelf!

Human knowledge has increased so enormously that no one can hope to keep up with it in detail. But it is important to have at least a general idea of what is going on. This can be accomplished quite effectively through a well-rounded reading program based on select books and magazines.

What has been said of intellectual development generally is true of the intellectual side of faith. "In understanding be men," the Scripture commands (I Corinthians 14:20). This is no contradiction with what has been said earlier: that it is impossible to find God by the intellect. Reason alone cannot produce faith, but once faith has been exercised, the mind can amplify and explore it.

Bible study is the chief means of realizing this purpose, but there are also theology, church history and dozens of other areas of religion. We should pay particular attention to understanding the essential doctrines of the Christian faith and our own denominational beliefs and practices. "Be ready always to give an answer to every man that asketh you a reason of the hope that is in you with meekness and fear" (I Peter 3:15).

But the needs of the mind go far beyond the purely intellectual. The whole area of culture is involved: music, art, drama, literature. To many Americans, culture is highbrow, egghead. They honestly don't like these activities and therefore avoid them. Others dislike cultural activities but endure them only for prestige reasons. Actually, for most people, culture is an acquired taste, gained by practice mingled with understanding. Today a person can easily take advantage of the many "appreciation courses" offered to assist in cultural development. Mastery of a new area of culture enriches life immensely and is wonderfully satisfying for the hungry ego.

It is true that mental progress is largely individual even when it occurs in collaboration with others, but much personality advance cannot be achieved alone. It is a function of living with others. Ego satisfaction depends on success in the endless competition between personalities — in other words, the achievement of leadership.

Unless a person is particularly ambitious, progress in this area faces the same two *devils* mentioned above, fear and laziness. Striving for leadership means putting ourselves in competition with others, with the accompanying and obvious danger of failure. The easiest way to avoid getting a bloody-nosed ego is not to stick your ego out. But since the personality is not content with the status quo, the anguish we avoid this way comes to us in a much worse fashion — the agony of rot. On the positive side, the pleasures of success are not for the fainthearted. On the other hand, laziness sidetracks the unpleasantness of effort, but quickly causes us to drift into the same evils as lack of courage.

The potential of leadership is enhanced by belonging to organized groups: church, service clubs, civic organizations, social groups, professional societies, political parties and the like. Most communities offer an almost endless variety to suit every whim.

Zest Instead of Insipidity

Even though man is essentially a social animal, merely *belonging* is not enough. We have to be active, doing our part, to make the group realize its objectives. Belonging to a group, which succeeds in making a worthwhile contribution to society, gives a similar satisfaction to personal success, because we identify ourselves with our groups.

Unfortunately, the path to leadership is thorny. We are surrounded at all times by petty personalities, and *we* are never entirely free from that vice ourselves. This means we will be hurt many times. Often our leadership will be opposed, not because our policies are wrong but simply because they are ours! The easiest thing to do is to get disgusted and quit. Personality mastery is achieved by taking all this opposition without resorting to personal reprisals, for it involves the skill of handling imperfect people. Leading a group of angels would, no doubt, be pleasant, but it would hardly present much challenge.

It was mentioned early in the chapter that a great deal of the joy of childhood comes from its endless variety, the newness of living. Since the normal circumstances of adulthood do not offer diversity, we have to seek out variety personally. Most people achieve this through the pursuit of worthwhile hobbies. Fortunately, this does not require too much ingenuity. Countless books cover the area and hobby shops are loaded to the ceiling with possibilities.

Most hobbies involve skills. Many call for developing skills with the hands. This mastering of new techniques and achievement is highly satisfying to the personality. Witness the pride with which a man calls in his wife to see a piece of furniture he has made!

In suggesting that a person, depressed through personality rot, should take up a hobby, I am frequently answered with the remark: "I can't seem to find anything I am interested in."

ABOVE OURSELVES

This is a little like the donkey that starved to death because no one particular bundle of hay appealed to him. You can't expect lightning to strike just by looking at a hobby from the outside. Often the most uninteresting tasks become absorbing when you get your hands into them. If you can't choose, toss a coin, but get started on something!

Keeping the Magic in Marriage

4

Keeping the Magic in Marriage

In our day, marriage counseling has become big business. Desperate couples wistfully seek out counseling services, ministers and psychiatrists, yearning for the magic formula that will save them from the heartache of divorce. Sometimes, not even an oracle could rescue them, for the cancer of bitterness and misunderstanding has spread to the heart. At other times the new understanding that comes from one who can view things impartially and objectively from the outside, restores the spell of romance again.

Unfortunately the demand for this kind of help is so heavy it is frequently difficult to obtain an appointment with a counselor, but don't be too discouraged if help is not immediately available. Honest self-examination and thoughtful soul-searching will aid in restoring marital happiness, however, just eliminating the symptoms is not enough. Unless the basic disease is treated, trouble will quickly reappear in other directions. That disease is generally the souring of one, or both, of the personalities through personal unfulfillment.

You may not be inclined to believe this. You may feel it is your husband's neglect, or your wife's nagging that is rubbing you raw. Strange isn't it how we are always ready to transfer blame to the other person. There is no denying that these objective faults do exist. But all personalities have faults to one extent or another. The deciding factor is not the fault, but the degree of irritation it causes. This, in turn, is not determined merely by how bad the fault is but *by how satisfied we are inside.*

When, in the course of a counseling session, a woman rehearses in vivid detail her husband's shortcomings I often wince, because my wife could justly complain about many of the same things in me, but she doesn't. Happily, she is completely involved in living an absorbing and satisfying life, but, if for any reason she should lose this fulfillment, she immediately would become painfully aware of my faults.

This is what is known as projection. The shadow of our own unhappiness is thrown on the other person and we imagine that the shadow is the reality causing all the grief. To use another illustration, the anguish of our unsatisfied personalities colors the glasses of our perception so that we see the frailties of the husband or wife in darker colors than they really are.

Observe what happened to Mary. For the umpteenth time her husband, Harry, was late for dinner. It would have been so easy for him to telephone but he didn't. In her mind Mary felt this showed he didn't feel she was important enough for this courtesy, and as the clock hands crawled around she became violently angry.

Just as his car came into the drive the telephone rang. It was a telegram informing her that a story she had sent to a major magazine had been accepted for publication. She grabbed the astonished Harry and almost smothered him with affection. He never knew how close he had come to being roasted alive instead.

You see, Mary's ego received a tremendous boost and her husband's fault now seemed insignificant. Now, of course, Harry cannot expect breaks like this all the time. He had better get on the ball himself. Neither can Mary count on more shots of adrenalin like that, but if she can raise the general level of her own ego-satisfaction, the result will be almost the same.

At first sight, this line of reasoning may not seem quite fair. On the surface, most of us tend to feel that Mary should do something about Harry's faults. He ought to be the one to straighten out. But this misses the point. What does she want? The satisfaction of rubbing Harry's nose in his misdemeanors or a happy marriage? Probably there is little she can do directly to reform Harry anyway, but she can learn to live with him in spite of his faults.

Actually it is because each individual spirit craves achievement that marriage is so difficult. By its very nature, it places restrictions and limitations on the personalities of both partners.

A man and his wife had just had a furious quarrel. He buried his head in the paper and she subsided into quiet sobbing. Between them on a mat by the hearth the dog and the cat lay peaceably, quite undisturbed by the mortal storm. The woman looked down at them and said pathetically: "Why can't we be like them?"

He raised his eyes from the paper to see what she was talking about and then snarled, "Yeah! But you tie their tails together and see what happens!"

At first this ego tension in marriage may not be noticed. It is swamped in the overwhelming emotion of the new experience. But when the emotion dies down, troubles start. A vague feeling of irritation inside triggers off lover's spats and later bickering and serious quarrels.

The usual alibi for these personality assaults is that "they clear the air," from which it is implied that quarrels are somehow salutary. This is a myth. Fights *always* do harm. Because of human frailty we are not going to avoid them entirely, but let's not fool ourselves by imagining they are blessings in disguise.

Even the magic of the romantic love of marriage can be dangerous for it drives the couple toward too much oneness. Oneness is wonderful if it doesn't go too far. If it does, it can choke the personality, and ultimately the spirit within begins to explore its way out! You can't hold it in for long.

The secret of happy marriage calls for a unique accomplishment. We must find the satisfaction of complete personal achievement within the limits proscribed by marriage itself and the impingement of the spouse's personality.

Romance and married love can make an immeasurable contribution to human happiness but only if the basic personality needs are met first. Lasting marital contentment is only for those who, independently of marriage, are realizing their maximum potential. When this is the case, there are no sore points in the personality to be rubbed raw by the myriad contacts of married life.

At 35, Vera had reached the stage when she just couldn't stand the sight of her husband. When asked what the difficulties were she had a list as long as your arm: he left his clothes lying around, he would leave the faucets to drip, he dozed in an armchair instead of mowing the lawn, he wouldn't discipline the kids, he was dull, lazy and sloppy. She was vaguely thinking of divorce, but her sense of responsibility wouldn't let her proceed.

She was a woman of considerable intellectual ability but had dropped out of school because of an early marriage. Deep down, the unfulfilled dreams were still there. After some prodding, she decided to go back to school. It's been hard looking after a family and taking a heavy academic load too, but now she's happier than she has ever been. Not only do her husband's inadequacies not seem so bad, but she is finding in him unsuspected qualities that are fine and good. The marriage has improved and is getting better all the time.

Vera will find that what nagging could not do, her example of a satisfying life can. Her increased alertness and richness of mind will challenge her husband. He'll grow with her.

Petty bickering is much more serious than most people realize. It is a symptom of frustration within. One becomes obsessed with the tiny things only when he hasn't anything big enough to capture the imagination.

This is where a renewal of vital religious experience can solve many of the problems in one great step. God gives a man something so big to live for that he no longer has any interest in petty griping. A woman discovers such a passion for Christ that all her personal relationships are transformed.

This doesn't mean that religion is an automatic cure-all. Religious people are plagued with marital troubles, too. It is not the amount of religion but the vital quality of the experience that counts. A man and a woman who are totally committed to Christ and His way of life, who are utilizing creatively their talents and abilities, are assured of a successful and happy marriage.

Prayer can be a powerful force in sore marriage relations, if it brings the couple to that place of surrender to the purposes of God and they become willing to forget their selfishness. But we cannot expect God miraculously to solve the problems or suddenly make our partner over so that he or she becomes as plastic clay in our hands. God respects personality and He does not bypass it or violate it. His Spirit will woo us toward the right but He will not force us. He wants to help us help ourselves.

At times religion can be a hindrance to harmony in marriage. One day a man brought his wife for counseling because things were in a desperate state. He was a minister and really didn't want counsel. Actually, he wanted me to persuade his wife to knuckle under, quoting liberally from Scripture about the wife obeying the husband and all that. According to him this was authority for him to act like a petty oriental monarch.

He was reminded that the Scriptures commanded that a husband should love his wife as Christ loves the Church.

"Do you treat your wife like Christ treats the Church?" He hung his head. But he still wanted the last word.

"What you don't know is that she's fallen in love with another man."

Tearfully she admitted it was true.

"We haven't committed sin," she said. "I know it is wrong but I couldn't help it. I haven't had a kind word from my husband in years. When this man started showing kindness to me, I couldn't resist."

Since the minister had set the pace for Scripture quoting, I had another verse for him: "Let him who is without sin among you cast the first stone."

It is doubtful that he was convinced. He's had all the answers for many years. But who knows?

Instances like this are sad. Nothing is more clear in the Bible than the responsibility to respect the personalities of others, to be gentle with them, to seek to bring about their emergence by unselfish love and kindness. Yet at times the same Scriptures are used as an excuse for personality murder.

There is no doubt that the Scriptures do teach that a man has the leadership role, that a woman's place is subordinate. This is good psychology, too, because women are not really happy in marriage any other way, but this is not an automatic right that a husband simply assumes. He has to earn this privilege, not by domination, but by creating an atmosphere of such personal satisfaction for the wife that she knows she can safely trust her happiness in his hands.

Keeping the Magic in Marriage

A battle for rights is one of the saddest things that can happen in marriage — sad because of failing to see the forest for the trees. The goal of marriage is happiness, not the fleeting upsurge that comes from a cheap personality victory. *You can win the right and lose the marriage.*

According to the Christian view there is something greater than exercising one's right — the privilege to waive those rights. It is often the best common sense.

Imagine you are approaching an intersection in your Volkswagon and you see a huge truck approaching from your left. The right-of-way is yours but if you insist on it you may not only be right, you may be dead right.

In marriage, negativeness, or counter-suggestion, can be brutally exasperating. One night the husband says: "Let's go out to eat tonight."

"Go out to eat? Do you think I rest all day? I'm tired. In the evening I need to rest, not go gallivanting around town."

The next night he tries a different line.

"Let's stay home tonight. It's nice and cozy here."

"Stay here?" she rasps. "Don't I get any consideration! I'm stuck in this place all day. A woman likes to go out once in a while."

But it isn't as illogical as it appears. Either because of her husband's domineering or because of her own personality defeats, her ego is sore and wounded. In its blind drive toward satisfaction it clutches at any straw — in this case the cheap victory of beating down another person's suggestions.

Counter-suggestion need not be conscious at all. It may be the involuntary reaction of the unconscious mind. This may make it more excusable but it doesn't make it any more pleasant.

Ego conflict is often the cause of unfaithfulness. This is especially true in women. After years of neglect and being

47

taken for granted, suddenly someone becomes interested in her as a person. No matter how shocking this is to her moral sensibilities, it is infinitely satisfying to her ego. It isn't sex that is basically important; it is the feeling of being wanted and appreciated.

The husband who is habitually involved in extramarital adventures has the same trouble. These Casanovas are not oversexed. Often they are quite inadequate sexually. They simply have no sense of self-confidence — no feeling of personal adequacy, so in a futile effort to "prove themselves," they move from one shoddy affair to another. It never works. The only way to find poise and confidence is from the inside.

Marital frigidity is often a notable symptom of ego problems. A woman may receive enormous personality satisfaction by giving herself to her husband, if she is the one who is doing the giving. On the other hand, if he arrogantly demands his "rights" with no thought for her feelings, obviously her ego suffers. In feeling that she is apparently no more than a sexual convenience, her unconscious mind recoils in disgust, and the result is frigidity.

However, with other women, frigidity may occur when a man fails to be masterful and demanding. She may feel inadequate because her husband is not awakened to violent heights of passion.

The point is that no married person can take the sexual life for granted. It is far from being a mere physical thing, but it is inextricably entwined with the emerging personality. There is no royal road — there are no pat answers, but as each person seeks to help his partner to greater self-discovery, the marriage relationship assumes its greatest dimension. If the personality factors in sexual life make the husband or wife feel "like a million dollars" there is not likely to be much of a physical problem.

Often money is a common cause of contention in marriage. This occurs in wealthy people as well as poor, so it is not merely the lack of money that causes trouble. Here again, the root cause is lack of respect for personality needs.

Many a husband considers his income as *his* because he earns it and this gives him the right to dole it out penny-by-penny to his dependent wife. It is easy to imagine how this makes the wife feel!

Both in law and in morals the income belongs to both. The husband has no more right to make significant expenditures without consulting the wife than the wife has without conferring with him. It is important to decide first how the money is to be spent and by whom. Then there should be no further interference.

In a counseling session we advised the husband to give his wife a fixed and adequate grocery allowance.

He said: "I do, but still she is not satisfied."

She replied: "He gives me an allowance all right and then he wants to know how I spend every penny of it."

Needless to say, the husband was strongly advised to keep his hands off that allowance. What she did with the money was completely up to her. A woman has to feel trusted and competent within mutually agreed upon guide lines.

The same is true in relationships with children. Nothing is more confusing to children and more detrimental to marriage than lack of distinct common policy. It should be clearly determined who will speak in the family in given situations. Occasionally the wife or husband may do something with which the other doesn't agree. But he or she must still back this action and present a united front to the children. Nothing is more galling to a person than to be contradicted and countermanded in the presence of the child.

Attention to this matter of the wife's personality feelings

can also save a lot of grief in connection with one of the big problems of modern life: how to spend enough time at home. Business and professional life is demanding enough upon a husband's time, but when civic duties are added, there are just not enough hours to go around, it seems.

Although not much can be done about this in the objective sense, the husband can lessen the feeling of neglect by using to advantage the time he does have at home.

For instance, husband, when you come in for dinner, don't just kiss your wife in a perfunctory manner, or grunt an incomprehensible monosyllable of greeting, and then retire behind the evening paper. Greet her warmly, smile into her eyes, watch for innovations in dress or hair upon which to compliment her, tell her how nice the house looks, ask her what has happened during the day. By your attentiveness make her feel good. Then if you have to go out in the evening you are not as likely to have a scene on your hands. You haven't given her any more time but you have made the most of what you do have to give her.

We have seen that almost any marital trouble can be traced to failure to accomplish personality achievement and recognition on the part of either the husband or wife or both. It is certain that if either partner is failing in his personal life, this will soon be projected on the marriage and may proceed to wreck it. On the other hand, by failing to allow adequate personal expression or by neglect and abuse, the marriage itself may be the cause.

No manual can give detailed instructions on how to mend every malfunction. Basic concepts can be discussed, but a happy marriage is the result of applied skill, understanding, love and common sense.

Marriages were designed by the Creator to be happy. Attentive human engineering can keep them that way.

How to Live With Children

5

How to Live
With Children

Nowhere is human behavior more bewildering than that observed in children. Yet nowhere is the mastery of human behavior more important. Formed in the image of God, the powerful inner forces of a child's mind and body are incomprehensible to them, and without adult understanding and guidance, they don't have a chance.

At first sight the problem appears to be enormously complicated. Each child is a unique individual; even so-called "identical twins" are vastly different. Treatment that brings beneficial results in one, may bring rebellion in another.

Some of us have already discovered this through trying experiences. When the first child arrived in our home, my wife and I made the usual blunders. We salved our bruised feelings in the delusion that we would master the art of child understanding with this child, and then apply our hard-earned psychology on the next one. Then, when the second boy came, he was so very different that we had to start all over. All six have been like that. It's probably just as well we didn't know this at the beginning.

Yet, in all this diversity there is one underlying principle that is always the same. Deep in the personality a tiny ego is starting its journey toward fulfillment. Everything that happens in the future, for good or bad, will inevitably be related to this.

Its first expression is naked and unashamed. The child is unshakable in his conviction that the universe revolves around him personally, and that every human being is his slave. He is completely oblivious to the inconvenience his behavior brings to others. Somehow we cudgel the ego into some semblance of civilization, but caged and controlled, at heart it remains the same. As long as there is life in the body, the ego never lets up in its endless quest to find its place in the sun.

At first it seems the child would be healthiest and happiest in an atmosphere of untrammelled self-expression. Actually the psychology of a generation ago advocated this idea.

Years ago, a professor of mine said: "If your child is crawling along the floor and comes into reach of your tablecloth, on which your best china is proudly displayed, don't hurt his personality by dragging him away. What is a few hundred dollars' worth of china anyway in comparison with his happiness?"

Of course, this attitude was stupid, to say the least. Apart from the fearful economic cost of such behavior, it did not satisfy. It was blind and purposeless expression. Self-assertion satisfies only when it is geared to meaningful achievements.

Yet how fearfully wrong was the common platitude that a child was like plastic clay in the hands of the parent. All you had to do was to mold him wisely, and mature, responsible adulthood would be the assured result!

What child was ever like that? His personality is as effervescent as his wriggling body. He is still only when asleep, and even then his mind goes on to weave a thousand fantasies. Far from being plastic, he resists even the slightest attempts of change.

On the other hand, parents cannot be objective sculptors anyway. Our egos have a stake in this game, too. A great deal of our own personality satisfaction is involved in this struggle which we call parenthood. When we succeed in getting him to obey, we feel like kings, but when he is defiant, we are filled with anger and frustration. The result is anxiety on our part, not only for him, but for ourselves.

School report cards reveal our true colors! The child comes home with a row of "F's." We convince ourselves that our dismay is purely objective — that we are only concerned about his future, but what we really think is something like this:

"His teachers will think the kid is stupid, and I'm his parent. Like father — like son. They'll think I'm stupid, too!"

Obviously we'll never get far as human engineers in this matter of parenthood until we recognize the stark fact that we are involved in an ego war. When two or more personalities are striving for fulfillment in the same environment, and at the expense of the other, a struggle is inevitable.

This phrase, ". . . at the expense of the other," seems crude and unfeeling, so requires some explanation. By their very love for the child, parents are often compelled to limit or modify the full expression of his ego. This is done, not to dominate, but to guide the immature child toward the achievement of worthwhile goals. Resistance by the child to this process creates a sense of parental failure that is released only by those high moments of acceptance and agreement.

The child also has goals, and these can only be realized by bending the parent's will, or at the expense of the parent's ego.

It is obvious that this conflict is inherent in the very nature of parenthood. It cannot be eliminated, although it can be minimized. Better still, it can be harnessed to give greater personality satisfaction in the long run.

The presence of this conflict has no bearing on the affection between parent and child. The child may love his mother dearly even while he is trying to outwit her. This is a source of guilt. Victories always hurt the other person, and when you hurt the person you love, you feel badly about it. This explains much of the mixed and changing emotions in a child.

Such conflict is not necessarily overt, although it frequently is. In anger, a child will often deliberately seek revenge against his parent, but at times the hostility is deep in his unconscious mind. Here it may trigger highly unpleasant behavior.

> Take Terry, for instance. After years of being completely housebroken, he suddenly developed the bedwetting habit. His mother was disgusted and shocked, a feeling which she showed in no uncertain manner when the first accident occurred.
>
> "You filthy little thing!" she said, as she dragged him violently from the bed.

It was this display of emotion which proved her undoing. Until then the little fellow had not been having much success in his ego struggle with his domineering mother. Now, by accident, he had found a weapon which could inflict the most obvious distress. His unconscious mind latched on to this like a gift from heaven, and the result was a compulsive habit.

When the mother was brought to understand this mechanism, she changed her domineering ways. She was careful to assume an attitude of near indifference to the bed-wetting incidents. When they ceased to produce any evidences of distress, the compulsion began to die out.

The twelve-year-old daughter of a minister developed a swearing compulsion. The first incident was quite innocent. She didn't even know what the word meant. But the embarrassment and shock of her father was only too evident. From that moment, no matter how much she tried to conquer the habit, the expletives would just pop out.

It isn't difficult to visualize the situation here. Unconsciously, the child resented the restraints of being a minister's daughter. The swear words provided an easy personality victory.

How to Live With Children

Recently some studies have indicated that poor grades from intelligent children were due to excessive aggressiveness on the part of the parent. It all adds up to the same story: the family situation is a battleground for ego war.

Since the build-up of this psychic tension is unavoidable, the only thing we can do is to attempt to neutralize it. The explosiveness of this tension must always be directly proportionate to the ego difference between parent and child, at least from the point of view of the child. To lessen this, there can only be two alternatives: to lower the parent ego, or raise the ego of the child. If we can achieve both, this is better still.

The parent can achieve his part by getting rid of all affectation and the tendency to "pull rank." Too often the parent, belittled by the circumstances of everyday life, or frustrated by his station in life, will compensate by acting like an oriental monarch at home. He may demand affection and allegiance as a parental right. He may be bad tempered, belligerent and domineering. He may be proud and arrogant. If so, he is simply asking to be brought down a peg or two, and believe me, the child is just the one to accomplish it.

There is much good psychology in the Biblical command: "Provoke not your children to wrath." It isn't the mere needling that does this, but a fundamental failure to respect the personality of the child.

Humility can be a great help in overcoming this problem. It is the grace to admit being wrong, the charity to overlook mistakes, the generosity to concede defeat in argument, the honesty to disclaim infallibility. If we voluntarily get down off the pedestal, there is no temptation to anyone to drag us off.

This attitude on the part of the parent is not merely a matter of mental discipline. It should be natural and unforced, and it will be, if we are personally living satisfying lives. When we descend to seeking cheap and petty personality victories over our children, we are in bad shape indeed.

The other approach to the problem is to lessen the ego difference between child and parent by helping the child to a higher level of achievement.

Actually, the child is confronted with a dual problem. He may be feeling bad because of failures, which put him behind in competition with others, or he may be frustrated because of constant mediocrity.

Poor or failing grades may be an example of the first problem. The reaction of parents, school and community to scholastic failure is now quite violent. In either case the consequent punishment to the ego is thus severe.

In itself, this reaction is not bad. It may prove a powerful stimulant to remedy the situation, but it is disastrous if the child finds himself in a blind alley. This will occur if his failure is due to faulty groundwork in the past, or because he just doesn't understand the work. It is important to counsel carefully with the teachers and others concerned, so that the problems can be remedied.

At times the problem may be compounded because the child just doesn't have the I.Q., or perhaps is lacking in a particular aptitude. This difference may occur within the same family.

For example, Ted comes home with a poor report card, while his younger sister, Joan, has one that is "all A's." The praise of the family causes her to glow with a sense of achievement, while Ted wants to find a hole in which to bury himself. Before long, he finds he has an almost ungovernable desire to clobber his sister. If he can't equalize things by scholastic endeavor, he will attempt to do so by physical violence.

Actually, Ted just doesn't have the mental equipment to compete with Joan. The only thing the parents can do is to guide him into other activities where he can excell. If he achieves in band, shop or sport, he will have found fulfillment.

Then his difference with his sister will be that of kind and not of degree.

The problem of ego satisfaction is directly proportional to personality endowment. The child who has great potential finds it hard to put all this to work. What is not usefully employed will spill over into mischief. This is why many great men were troublemakers when they were children.

So, if your child is a perfect angel, don't congratulate yourself too quickly. It may be that he is either not too richly endowed or else he is storing up his frustrations for some future explosion! On the other hand, don't be too discouraged if your youngster has problems. This is to be expected in a child with ability. However, don't be complacent either — if he doesn't realize his potential, it will break loose somewhere.

You don't choose a racehorse for his mildness. A docile animal won't give any trouble, but he won't run any races either. The spirited horse may be hard to "break," but he will be worth all the discipline in the long run.

Good discipline is that kind of guidance which trains the child to control his energies and express them effectively. If we don't succeed in getting internal discipline for the child, all our external discipline will be useless.

We often speak nostalgically of the good old days of stern, parental, corporal punishment, but this discipline is far from being what it is cracked up to be. It is true that many a boy is improved by being belabored at times in the place where it is felt the most, but as a general rule, physical violence will merely toughen the delinquent. Such punishment is an offense against his own personality.

The truth is that there is no easy solution to the discipline problem, but if the child has confidence in his parent and if the parent himself is disciplined, the chances are it will be reproduced in the child.

The relation of parents, one to another, vitally affects ego tranquility in a child. If he is the victim of a home where parents bicker, or if the home is broken up entirely, he feels he has been robbed. It is obvious to him that his parents think more of themselves than they do of him.

The child needs to be loved in the New Testament sense of the word. This is far more than mere affection. It is the knowledge that the parents consider his welfare more important than their own. He needs to be constantly reassured on this point by both word and action.

Now, this book is not intended to give specific solutions to specific problems. Human nature is far too complicated for this. No problem is ever reproduced in exactly the same way. But it isn't necessary to treat a behavior crisis by trial and error. In almost every case, the problem will boil down to the fact that the child's realization of his personality powers is being hindered or blocked in some way. A step toward the solution is to find out exactly what is causing the frustration.

Unfortunately, an understanding of the basic psychology involved is only part of the task. Otherwise those of us who are trained in clinical psychology would be the best parents, and this is not particularly true. Of far greater importance is the skillful implementation of corrective means, after you find out what is wrong. This can't be learned from books. Some parents seem to have a touch of genius in this area, even though they can't read or write. To most of us, experience is the only real teacher.

Our discussion so far has been geared to techniques. But it should not be forgotten that what we *do* is of little value in comparison with what we *are*. Between people who live together and love each other, there is a steady interpenetration of personalities. Whether we like it or not, we induce ourselves, for good or ill, into the life of the children.

Pretense is worse than useless. It is what we are that gets

through, not what we say. Our children become copies of ourselves.

Therefore, it is of the utmost importance that we exemplify what we teach. Our children cannot be expected to find the good life unless they see it in us.

Then again, children tend to identify themselves with us. If we lack integrity, and are the victims of moods and temper — inadequate in personality — the prey of bad habits, they will feel as ashamed as if they themselves were in our shoes. This crushing blow to the ego can only result in violent compensating behavior.

To be a good parent is to be a good person, or at least one who is sincerely trying. Remember, God is far more interested in our success than we are, and His guidance is constantly at our disposal. It won't come like a voice out of the blue, but it will be there — a gentle pressure upon the heart and the mind, as we seek to do the right thing in unselfish love and quiet understanding.

Reaching the Teenager

6

Reaching the Teenager

In the Sermon on the Mount Jesus spoke of the blessedness of the meek (Matthew 5:5). As it appears in the English translation, we find this attribute of human goodness quite unattractive. But the derivation of the Greek word really means something like our word "controlled." It refers to strength which has been controlled for useful purposes. There is nothing passive in the idea at all. It stands for energy, disciplined and directed toward satisfying achievement.

This is the secret of the maturing of the teenager. It is as much a mistake to break his spirit as it is to let it run wild. The trick is to harness it. (I will call the young person "him" for simplicity but the principles for girls are just the same.)

Learning to control the powers within requires time and patience on the part of the teenager. At times he hurts himself, at times he hurts others. Sudden successes may go to his head and make him temporarily unmanageable. He will make all the mistakes in the book. But even the worst misadventures may not be as disastrous as we might think. This is his way of finding himself.

Unfortunately, the process of maturing is largely blind. We may long to offer him our advice and at times we will experience frustration when we're brushed off. His behavior is not determined by logic but by emotional and personality forces within him. Probably we've forgotten, but we were the same when we were young.

It is significant that most great men had their troubles during youth. Many of them even failed in school. In some cases their parents died heartbroken over their erring ways. Something of this has to be expected. After all, in the world of machines we also have to be careful how we handle a 250-horsepower engine, too.

We may be encouraged by the thought that human progress is seldom a steady advance without setbacks — more like the incoming tide in which the wavelets ebb and flow. This is especially true of the adolescent. We must learn not to be too discouraged by the troughs or too encouraged by the crests. More important still, we must not infect the teenager with our dismay or our complacency. He must see that we have faith in his success.

It may be hard for us to understand, but even his most bizarre behavior is perfectly explicable. This does not mean that it is excusable! But it is his inexperienced, and sometimes frantic, way of finding expression for the powers that he is experiencing inside.

We have seen that even a child is motivated by the drive of his personality for expression, for satisfaction, for fulfillment, for recognition. But during the childhood years, because of the relative strength of the parents' will as against that of the child, we can keep him within bounds, even if we fail to satisfy his ego needs. But when adolescence comes, that parental advantage begins to slip away. For one thing his personality powers explode into adulthood and may match our own. For another, his will may be as strong as ours, or stronger. The time inevitably comes when he is beyond the reach of forceful parental sanction altogether. Fortunately we can still reach him in other ways.

There is a new factor added to the power of the emerging

ego in adolescence and that is the promise of independence. He begins to take on some of the self-sufficiency of adulthood. There is a yearning to find his own place in the sun. He still loves his parents but must live his own life.

This is hard for parents. He has been a personal satisfaction to us throughout the years of childhood. As we see him begin to mature, we want to clutch him to us and hold him forever. Some parents actually attempt this. The result is disastrous. The young person struggles to free himself to retain his freedom and self-respect and is ravaged with guilt when he sees the pain he is causing. If we not only let him go but even aid him in his drive for independent personal fulfillment, we will find that the relationship, though different, is closer than ever.

One teenage girl had a very unhappy adolescence. It was a sad story of rebellion and recrimination between her and her mother, all the more painful because their affection for each other was real and deep. Then, much against the mother's will, the girl got married. Fortunately at that point, the mother bowed to the inevitable and withdrew. Now they are completely happy. The bickering and quarreling have gone. They respect each other as two independent persons.

It is obvious that we have a responsibility to move the teenager along toward adult freedom at the fastest possible rate consistent with his own development. Of course, we must not abdicate our parental responsibility in the process. Unlimited freedom before he is ready for it would be disastrous. This is not only true because of the trouble he may get himself into but because he may interpret this as being evidence that we don't care. This is damaging to his ego and his behavior will quickly reflect it.

But this mustn't be used as an excuse to prolong control over him. Most especially we avoid being over-protective. He has the God-given right to make his own mistakes and it would be tragic if we hedged him in so tightly that he was prevented from burning his fingers a little. But we don't have to let him chop his arm off, either.

If we stop to think about it, our imagination will run riot about the ways in which he can hurt himself. Accidents can occur at football, on his bicycle, in his car, on the streets and in a million other ways. The answer is not to prohibit him from engaging in anything that involves danger but to teach him how to take care of himself.

Probably the most frightening crisis of all is the time when the teenager gets old enough to drive a car. Teenage statistics being what they are, we die a thousand deaths whenever he is driving. We can't remove this peril altogether, but we can minimize it by providing him with driver's education or a commercial driving course. We can also insist that his driving privilege is conditional on a good record. If he begins to amass citations for traffic violations, the car should be taken away. Above all, we should be careful not to lump all teenagers together as "incorrigibles." Many are among the most skillful drivers.

The whole idea of maturation is the gearing of the degree of freedom with responsibility. We should make it clear to him that we are as eager to help him to independence as he is to achieve it, but that he must progressively earn it.

Take the problem of being out at night. It is important that from the start each event should be talked over beforehand and a suitable deadline for his return agreed upon. At first the hour will necessarily be early but it should not be just one particular hour regardless of circumstance. It should fluctuate according to whether the next day is a school day or a weekend and also on the nature of the function. We should let him know that the agreed-upon deadline is not to be altered except upon exceptional circumstances. As additional responsibility is assumed, he can be given freedom to stay out later.

Incidentally it should be said here that we should always know where he is. When he goes out at night, it should always be to *specific* places. If he is allowed to wander the streets at random with nothing particular in mind, the result will be trouble even with the best of young people.

Perhaps the worst feature of this journey to independent adulthood is the head-on collision between the parent and the young person. Some of these are inevitable, but they are nevertheless disastrous. The parent may win but the blow to the young person's self-assurance and the wounds to his ego are serious. He will now be in a sullen and rebellious mood, poised for the opportunity to avenge himself. Of course, the result may be even worse: the teenager may win!

It is wise to be on the alert for these storms as they appear on the horizon and head them off before they can do any damage.

If a clash becomes inevitable we can save a lot of unpleasantness by remaining calm and dignified. We will be tempted to win a cheap and easy victory by demolishing his arguments outright. But we are here to help him and not use him as a foil in a personality war. Let's hear him out and appraise his situation as calmly as we can, then act decisively but sympathetically. Above all, we must not argue or become involved in a knock-down drag-out fight.

The problem is seldom intellectual anyway. Beneath the words, he is being torn by emotional needs. To make them acceptable he has to rationalize them and in his inexperience his logic is crude and his defense thin. If we really want to help him, we must seek for an understanding that probes beyond his verbalization. When we have to say "no" we still have a responsibility to meet his need in some other way.

If we realize this fundamental thesis that a teenager is an emerging personality striving for fulfillment, we will be able to see that his widely heralded sexual drive is quite secondary. Unfortunately he is growing up in a generation which has become somewhat obsessed with sex. Indeed, it sometimes acts as if sex has just been discovered for the first time. The adolescent is given the impression that he is facing a terrible danger which is enormously difficult to handle. With us, sex is so obtrusive, that he is talked into problems which otherwise would not exist.

If a young person is finding for himself an absorbing and a satisfying life he seldom is aware of undue pressure from sex. His desires are there and he is fully aware of them, but they do not become oppressive as long as ego energy is not channelled into them. If he becomes a failure or thinks he is a failure, or if his energies are not absorbed, then morbid sexual imagination will quickly take over.

Of course, he should know that sexual misadventure is wrong. No pleasure is worth the trouble if you can't bear the look of God into your own soul afterwards. No self-respecting fellow would rob someone else of something valuable even if he were gullible enough to let him. There is no satisfaction that way. Sex is only satisfying if it is a part of a permanent relationship which has the approval of God and man.

The appeal to the girl is somewhat easier because she has more to lose. The news of sexual misconduct spreads fast. Sometimes it only takes an incident to give the permanent reputation that she is "that" kind of girl. Since the girl is craving for recognition and social achievement, it means that if she understands these consequences, we will have human psychology on the side of morals.

It is most important that the teenager understand the difference between control and repression. So much has been said about the dangers of repression that sometimes the impression has been given that the only way to avoid mental disturbance is to give unbridled expression to sexual desire. The very reverse is true. The damage to the mind through immorality is intensive. Not even the most sophisticated can avoid it. Underneath, guilt festers and poisons. I have seen a man break down completely at 53 because of an indiscretion at sixteen. Promiscuity can produce sexual impotence or frigidity. Sometimes it makes subsequent marriage a nightmare.

Since marriage lags several years behind sexual maturation, self-denial and self-control are inevitable. But this is also good. It helps to put sinews into the personality. It aids in the mastery of the self, producing poise, strength and integrity.

Repression is a very different matter. It occurs when the adolescent is horrified by his sexual feelings, refusing to admit their existence, driving them out of sight into the unconscious. This is deadly.

Instead let him say to himself: "Sure I have sexual urges. I'd be a funny kind of person if I didn't. These are given to me by God, and there is nothing wrong with them."

A boy who is defeated by sex, or anything else for that matter, is a frustrated individual. The ego drive is such that he can only be contented when it is in control. In other words, human nature is really on our side, if we interpret it correctly and in line with the laws of God.

The "going steady" fad of recent years has contributed to the difficulty. It places the young person in an emotional and behavioral straitjacket long before he is ready for it. It falsely suggests rights to the other person's body and leads directly to sexual experimentation. In early adolescence, it should be discouraged.

The emotional stability required for faithfulness in marriage takes a long while to mature. When 16-year-old Sally is madly in love with John on Monday, but can't live without Peter on Wednesday, she isn't being fickle. She is perfectly normal. You can't force maturation. It has to come at its own rate.

Long engagements are to be discouraged because sexual

intercourse almost always becomes the practice after a while. The result is moral guilt and worry about pregnancy, and the psychological factors involved work to break up the relationship. To the boy, the sex act is the end of the hunt and often terminates the affection, and his ego will tend to drive him to start another conquest. In other words, the most direct way for a girl to lose her fiancé is to give in to him. By contrast, the sex act tends to crystallize the affection in a girl. Thus when the boy loses interest, she may be driven to suicide even, as the records unhappily show.

In time she may apparently get over it and marry someone else, but a feeling of love for her former fiancé may be buried deeply in her subconscious mind. I have seen a number of cases of marital frigidity caused by this, for the unconscious repressed love may inhibit her ability to mate with anyone else.

There is much to be said for the feeling in some countries that a man should not marry a girl until he has proved his love for her by making adequate financial provision. This tends to delay marriage until emotional maturity and at the same time remove one of the most destructive agents in marriage: money worries.

A common problem for parents of a teenager occurs when he falls in love with the wrong person. (Perhaps the feminine pronoun should be used here because the problem is most often that of the daughter interested in some undesirable boy.)

In such cases exert every effort to remain objective. Naturally we feel no one is good enough for *our* daughter, which, of course, doesn't give her much choice. It is also only too easy to be governed by prejudice and hearsay and thus do the boy a terrible injustice.

This is the worst time in the world to panic for we may drive her right into his arms. If there are some facts about him that she needs to know, let's tell her frankly without elaboration or nagging. Remember, a persistent barrage of verbal abuse about him will probably cause her to rise heroically to his defense.

Far better to say something like this: "Janie, you know we love you and want the best for you. But it's your life and what you do with it is up to you. We think you may be making a mistake here but it's for you to decide. In the long run, whatever you want, we are on your side."

This way she has only one factor to appraise: the boy himself. If he is worthless, the chances are she'll find it out. But if we are emotionally involved too, she won't be able to see the forest for the trees.

If it's a question of marriage, delay is a good test. Fortunately, the law is on our side here. The best way to handle this is by way of compromise. We can say something like this: "Okay. If you really want to marry him we'll go along, but if you are that sure you won't be afraid of putting this to the test of time. If you feel the same in six months you've proved your point and you have our blessing."

It may be that she will go ahead anyway. If that should happen, it pays to give in gracefully for her sake. Boycotting the wedding and disowning her would be stupid and un-Christian. She is going to need us all the more now. Painful though it may be to us, she has a right to make her own mistakes, just as we did (or do).

Young people all seem to have their sticky patches when nothing seems to go right. During these lows there may be a succession of problems and irritations. To the agonized parent it may seem that all that has been built up for years is falling apart. The young person is bewildered and lost. This is when the faith and confidence of the parents mean a great deal. If, instead of this, he senses panic he may react adversely and be driven by fear to foolish action.

Experience indicates that these rough spots are almost

always temporary anyway. Growing up personality-wise draws a tremendous amount of energy and, at times, the young person just "runs out of gas." His resistance is low and his motivation weak. Then, just as quickly as he falls into the slump he will jump out of it. He has replenished his energy and is ready to go. The wise parent, therefore, will refrain from acting as if the end of the world has come.

One of the most disturbing of these slumps is the dropping of motivation in school. The word "dropping" can be most realistic in this connection. One day he may be doing fine, the next totally disinterested. High grades may plunge to F's almost overnight. The teachers will complain that he has become listless and inattentive, even sassy. At home, he will lie about his homework, question the usefulness of his subjects or of high school in general. Counter argument about the necessity of education is brushed off with a sneer.

At these times we must watch our own personality involvement. If we slip into ego identification with him, we will feel personally disgraced. In our frustration we may be tempted to nag and abuse him but this will succeed in really muddying up the waters. If, instead, this is regarded as a mere case of "personality measles," we will be patient and more tolerant.

The best way to confront this problem is to find out all the facts first, by consulting the teachers, principal or counsellor and the coach. If we can get the boy to talk about his gripes, this will help. It may turn out that he has dropped behind in some area, or does not understand what he is doing, or has inadequate background. This will cause him to feel so insecure that he may seek to insure himself against defeat by not even trying. Remedial work could soon change all this.

But particular causes may not be evident at all. Then firmness and follow-through are indicated. We should make sure he does his homework by keeping a close contact with the school. It often helps to involve ourselves in his studies, asking questions about them and getting him to inform us. Experiments have shown that praise is a most effective motivation and we should use it lavishly.

The bitterest pill of all is the incidence of delinquency or an act of crime. Nothing can equal the agony of seeing one's own child arrested by the authorities and brought into the courts. But it can and does happen even in the best of families. Sometimes there is warning — more than often there is not. The reason for the violation seldom makes sense. Usually it is due to this same powerful ego driving for expression and now finding it in breaking through the barriers of the law. (The motivation slump in school is one common pre-indicator).

Many of these infractions are quite incidental and probably accidental too. But the results for the young person are always frightful. He may put on a blase facade but inside he is a terrified person. I feel it is helpful for the authorities to be very firm. But it is vital that he experience our love and understanding and continued acceptance *of him.* Any feeling of rejection can be tragic.

The final answer, of course, is to help him into a more satisfying life. If an adolescent has enough good things to absorb his attention, he is not likely to be sidetracked.

The greatest gift that we can give to our teenager is a vital religious faith. The power of God within will give him strength and purpose. It will draw out his inner powers and give him a medium for expression. It will harness his energies in cooperation with God in His work of redemption and give him a clear goal for all living.

But what has been said in the chapter on religion is most applicable here. Mere churchgoing or vague acquiescence will not help. His faith must be such a complete committal that it totally captures his imagination. It will then be applied with beneficial results to every area of his life. He may overdo some things in his enthusiasm but this is typical of youth. If he is sincere, it will not make him a fanatic.

Without such a strong religious faith, his life will have neither anchor nor purpose.

The best way to win him into such an experience is to introduce him to a group who are committed in this way. Emphasis on what he will get out of it will not be a good selling point but challenge to what he can do for God, even at great sacrifice, will attract him like a magnet. The sense of the heroic in youth is extremely strong.

Let's not undersell our modern youth. They are neither morally depraved, delinquent, nor irresponsible. They are the finest specimen of humanity the world has produced. All they need is to be shown something to live for.

Power to Persuade

7

Power to Persuade

Personal fulfillment can come only in relation to others. As we have seen, though the roots of satisfaction are within, man cannot live alone. His personality reaches for achievement in relation to people and craves for recognition by them. This means struggle and competition with the highest rewards for those who can persuade.

This struggle need not be the "nature red in tooth and claw" of Darwinian fame. Indeed, any such kind of vicious contest without regard for the feelings of the other person brings its own inevitable retribution. If we climb merely by stepping on others, we only succeed in raising up an army of people dedicated to dragging us down.

Recent studies have shown that the popular picture of the executive as a blustering tyrant riding roughshod over his underlings and competitors is largely erroneous. There are such men, but generally they do not last long. They raise too many personal problems. The modern successful executive is quiet, courteous, efficient, poised, sympathetic. His weapon is persuasion and not the big stick.

We have seen a similar change in salesmen. A generation ago it was the high-pressure hot sell — the personality bully with his foot jammed in the door. These methods made quick sales but they destroyed goodwill and killed repeat business. The present-day successful salesman shows respect for his customer's personality and attempts to build a future on his satisfaction.

The prime factor governing success is to recognize clearly the psychological problem which has been the basis of everything discussed so far. Each person with whom we have to deal is an emerging ego like ourselves. If we appear as a threat to his fulfillment, his entire nature will be mobilized to block us. If our association with him promises greater satisfaction for him, that same power will be on our side.

Now let us not imagine that there is any complete solution to this psychological problem. People who live together in the same community necessarily make demands upon one another. Though the result is some limitation of expression, the negative effects can be minimized and the power itself can be harnessed and directed toward success.

The most obvious requirement is that we must sell ourselves before we can sell *our products*. However, we won't sell ourselves unless we constitute genuine and attractive *products* in our personalities.

A few years ago I talked with a man who had lost his family and his job and whose soul was racked with bitterness. He complained that every prospective employer turned him down on sight. I told him I couldn't blame them. His face and personality were wrapped in eternal gloom. He was so touchy that he took offense at the slightest imagined provocation.

I urged him to develop a happy, smiling, confident demeanor when he went in for an interview.

"Are you asking me to be a hypocrite?" he asked.

"What do you mean?"

"I don't feel that way, so why should I put on a pretense?"

I tried to show him that there was another alternative. He could change inside!

This is where "techniques" of salesmanship often fail. You cannot put on a personality mask just for the occasion. To the discerning person, the deception is obvious. Even if we are clever enough to put on a successful act, it violates our own integrity and before long we wouldn't even believe in ourselves.

There is no substitute for genuineness and sincerity. To change oneself into a likeable *product* is a long hard job. It takes discipline and concentration, but it is the only way.

The more complete and satisfied persons we are in every area of life, the more we will be able to persuade. The reason why a prospect will allow himself to be persuaded by us when we are pleasant and complete persons rather than misfits, is identification. In contact with us he sees either people he would like to emulate or people whose image he wants to avoid. If it is the former, he will identify our *product* as contributing to that end and vice versa. Remember, he is straining for fulfillment too.

One telling aspect in the personality of the would-be persuader is self-confidence. There is good reason for this. The "common cold" of the personality is insecurity, so we can be sure that our contacts are suffering from it to some degree or another. If they see timidity or fear in us, we will look too much like themselves and they will be repelled. If they witness poise and strength, they will be drawn to us, for they are hungering for this too.

However, self-confidence is not false pride or bravado. That is mere whitewash. If we have self-confidence, it will be obvious. If we lack self-confidence, we can develop it by experience and maturity. It's going to be difficult at first, but as we succeed in persuading, we will automatically take on this kind of poise.

In spite of the fact that we are living a full and satisfying life, we may still negate this by unfortunate mannerisms. We are never safe from these, for they develop subtly and imperceptibly. A good, responsible wife is the best preventative. We should encourage her to point out these peculiarities as soon as they appear.

Effective powers of communication are, of course, vital if we are going to persuade. Obviously effective communication is the one way in which the message can be transmitted. Also, it is a factor in the reception of the message. If a presentation is clear, the listener tends to interpret this as a mark of his own intelligence. If it is foggy, he will blame the speaker, although he may have a nagging doubt that his own mental equipment is at fault.

Self-consciousness is probably the most common barrier to both private and public speech. Practice and experience are the only cures, but concentration on, and enthusiasm about, the *product* and the needs of the listener can change any stuttering failure into a glowing success.

In all areas of leadership it is important that the ego of the leader be kept unobtrusive, otherwise there will be ego war. Pride on the part of any person in a position of prominence will quickly nullify his influence. Humility will increase his power.

Incidentally, if humility is a personal problem with us, it isn't simply because we are too heavily loaded with intrinsic merit — it's because we are stone blind! Any person with the smallest element of perception can find enough wrong with himself to remain humble for a lifetime.

The ability to persuade is often hampered by a childish desire to show off or boast. The child shows off because in his inexperience, he is grasping at quick ego fulfillment through recognition, but he soon learns that he will be quickly slapped down. If our virtues and talents are really there, people will see them without our pointing them out.

I once saw an insurance sales manual which advised insurance men to gain goodwill in their communities by being active in civic affairs but to avoid positions of authority that might be envied. If this rule were always rigorously followed, the community and the church would suffer. But the manual does make a good point. The more we leave the plums to others, the more effective a job we can do in the art of persuasion. Others won't feel they have to knock us to make themselves look good. This principle is exemplified in the advice to hand out bouquets to others when a job has been well done. A leader may justly feel that since it was his brains, planning, initiative and drive that accomplished the task, he has a right to the accolades. This is maybe true, but it is poor policy and will cut his own throat in the long run. If one wants wholehearted support in the future, he'd better let the praise go to his subordinates. This recognition will be a personal satisfaction to them and they will want to follow him in the future with the hope of getting more of the same. People cannot be persuaded to follow your leadership unless they feel that this will be a fulfilling and rewarding experience.

Humor is a valuable device in minimizing this ego war. A great part of the psychology of laughter lies in the fact that it is an emotional satisfaction in relieving ego tension. Much situational humor depends on someone being belittled. This raises our egos relatively and makes us feel good in the process. Many of our funniest jokes relate to ministers, professors and those in authority (such as the President of the United States). By the nature of their jobs, these men exert a certain amount of authority over us. Intellectually we recognize the necessity of this, but it is always unpleasant to our egos. We get back at such figures of prominence through our jokes.

Public speakers often use this approach to gain rapport at the beginning of a speech. They know that the nature of their function arouses ego resistance, but if they belittle themselves by means of a personal experience, the resistance breaks down. Unconsciously the listeners feel that they have gained a point ego-wise on the speaker.

Negativism is another distressing symptom of ego war. Some people are against any proposal no matter how good. Since they are insecure and cannot achieve by themselves they find satisfaction only in blocking others. Strange as it may seem, this defect can be used advantageously. For example:

A young Baptist minister was anxious to get a much needed building program approved by his church, but there was one deacon who was of this negative disposition and his influence could be decisive. The minister went to him and said:

"I need your help. I'm new in this business and must rely on people of experience like you. I've come to you because you have more influence than anyone else in the church."

The old man glowed.

"Son," he said. "I'd be delighted to help."

"Well, sir," said the preacher. "I know that your heart must be just breaking with the need to have more space for the work of the Lord. So I thought I'd ask you to present our new building proposals to the church."

"Son," said the deacon, "you've come to the right man. You can count on me."

He got the building.

Unfortunately, our first reaction is to want to win a cheap ego victory by a head-on fight. It takes much more time and diplomacy to harness the opposing ego energy to our purposes, but it pays off in the long run, not only because we succeed in the project but because we give others fulfillment in the process.

Any organization will start to fall apart when the subordinates feel they are merely pawns in the game. It is the leader's task to make each person feel important and also feel their jobs are significant. In achieving this the leader will want to get to know each one personally, to know his family, his interests, his hopes, even his complaints. Expression of a personal interest in others is always a tremendous boost to their ego.

Most organizations have at least one troublemaker. The easiest way to solve the problem is to eliminate him. However, there may be times when this is both inhumane and unwise. The person may be simply drawing attention to an ego that is craving for expression. If we can get close to him and find out what's bothering him, we may be able to harness this wasted potential for useful purposes. This would remove the snag and add to the efficiency of the operation at the same time.

Years ago an old schoolmaster told me something that I will never forget:

"Jauncey, if you can teach the good ones, there's no credit in that. It's when you can teach the duds that you really succeed."

The challenge to persuasion and leadership is in the winning over of the problem people and the misfits.

If we are leading a project, its success may well depend on how good a selling job we do. Many leaders fail at this point because they fail to delegate authority. Frequently enthusiasm to do a good job may cause us to become overly involved in detail and actually interfere with the established function of other people. Their egos are wounded because they know they are not being trusted, and before long they are consciously or unconsciously working against us. Supervision may be necessary but it should always be unobtrusive. It should be more of the nature of follow-through then direct involvement.

Much of life is spent in persuading people about ideas: a religious message, a moral principle, a political platform, a civic duty, an article of truth, a course of action. Whether the attempt is made in private conversation or in a speech, we obviously cannot be successful unless we convince others that our ideas are vitally important. Human nature is such that we feel only the most important matters are worthy of our attention. It is, therefore, essential for the would-be persuader to be convinced that his message is vitally important before he starts to sell it. His reasons must be cogent and urgent.

An English minister was once chided by his deacons because every time he announced his sermon text he said it was the most important in the whole Bible. He wasn't being inconsistent. No one should attempt to communicate any message unless he considers it to be at that moment the most important message in the world. However, merely to verbalize its urgency is not enough — to be contagious, it must be deeply felt.

If a person is to be persuaded, he must sense personal identification, a cause or a need. If we are telling him about life insurance, the prospect must be made to visualize his own family in need at his untimely death. If we are expounding the dangers of socialism, he must see his own freedom in danger. If we are preaching the Gospel, he should be convinced of his own personal need. His vital interests have to be involved. The techniques to be used depend on the ingenuity of the salesperson, but one good way is the concrete example or illustration. For instance, the difference between a dry sermon and a live sermon may well depend on the vividness of the illustrations. We are challenged when we can identify with the message one way or another.

Furthermore, this ego principle demands decision and action as the result of having been persuaded. We are not interested when nothing is expected of us, but whenever someone is urging us to act or decide, our egos are instantly alert, for here is a possible opportunity for further fulfillment.

This does not mean pressing for premature action. If we are pressed for action before the truth of the matter is crystallized in our minds, we generally react against the persuader. We get the impression that instead of leading us into truth, he is simply interested in winning a personality victory over us.

Actually, our involvement is quite delicate. If the contact is not led to a decision when he is ready for it, he will feel badly let down. On the other hand, if he is hurried, he will be rebellious. In this kind of personality interplay you must develop an instinct for action. It pays to exert some pressure, yet be sensitive enough to another's feelings to know when to stop.

We can see that the art of persuasion is far more than use of eloquent words. It is the inter-involvement of two personalities, with the one leading the other into truth which has already been accepted by his whole being. It is an outreach of Christian love seeking to enrich and not degrade or defeat.

The art of persuasion and the gift of leadership are the same. There is no battle of wills, no dominance of one personality over another. Instead, the giver and the receiver find ego or personality fulfillment in the same experience.

The Nervous Breakdown

8

The Nervous Breakdown—
Causes and Characteristics

The nervous breakdown has become common to our day. This does not mean that it is new. It is as old as man, but it has increased in frequency. Few families go for a lifetime without being hit.

The term "nervous breakdown" refers to many degrees of illness — severe mental disease to temporary nervous debility. It may be characterized by a breakdown in emotional control, some loss of rationality, distortion in sense perception, black moods of depression, inability to make decisions, decreased control of physical movement, trembling, nervousness, headaches, weakness, etc. It often requires complete rest, usually an initial period of bed rest or hospitalization.

The causes of breakdowns are many, differing greatly from person to person. There is no unanimity of opinion as to whether the problem is basically physical, or mental and emotional. This is part of the age-old question of the relationship between mind and body. Over the past fifteen years psychiatry has appeared to reverse itself somewhat. For many years, under the influence of the psychoanalysts, it was almost axiomatic that conflict in the unconscious mind was responsible. Now there is substantial evidence that physical factors may also be involved. Actually the two approaches are not mutually exclusive. It is likely there is a constant interaction between emotional and physical causes so that therapy from either approach, or both, can be beneficial.

There appears to be renewed medical interest in the function of the endocrine glands in nervous disorders. This was considered quite probable a generation ago when some of us were in school. These endocrine glands excrete tiny quantities of hormones into the system, that have a powerful influence on the emotions and on behavior generally. When their rate of intake into the system is upset by injury, disease or malfunction, the results may be devastating. In such cases remarkable cures have been brought about by the use of synthetic hormones. It is quite possible that some unbalance in the endocrine function could be a contributing factor to many nervous breakdowns.

Excessive fatigue is often a factor, especially in mental fatigue. Such things as worry, conflict, tension or guilt, consume vast quantities of nervous energy. This may steadily eat into nervous capital until it is practically exhausted. Suddenly there simply isn't enough nervous energy left to control the impulses of the nervous system, or to control the emotions or the will. This action is much like that of an automobile battery. When it falls below a certain point, it just gives up entirely.

Then again, the nervous condition may be an outward symptom of a serious physical difficulty, such as a brain tumor. Consequently, counselors should insist that the person undergo thorough medical examinations before prescribing therapy.

Mental conflict is always at the roots of problems. The conflict can cause the affliction in two ways: either by using up the mental energy to the point of exhaustion, or by using the symptoms of the breakdown as a spurious satisfaction to the repressed inner needs.

Certain repressions so popular with psychology in the past are now fast losing favor. Sex is a case in point. Under Freudian psychology (or distortions of it) the repression of overt sexual behavior was felt to be particularly dangerous. So much so, that some analysts boldly advised patients to find relief by extra-marital sexual intercourse and ridiculed the religious and moral implications. Such a concept fails to square with the facts of human behavior. Sexual intercourse without a permanent love relationship *does not* satisfy, and guilt generated by the violation of ideals is much more serious than the tension of unsatisfied sexual desire.

The idea that sexual activity is essential to mental health is fallacious. Many people live celibate lives without tension. The energy which would normally go into this channel is sublimated. If this energy is used in a full and satisfying life, the sexual lack will be minimized. It is quite likely that worry or preoccupation about sexual abstinence is far more damaging than the abstinence itself.

Then again, there has been a tendency to overemphasize the importance of the "traumas" or shocks of childhood. Few people go through these formative years without damaging experiences which leave lasting scars. However, many people, whose childhood was little better than a hell on earth, achieve in adulthood the same kind of maturity and adjustment to living as those whose childhood was comparatively free from traumatic experience. On the other hand, it is quite possible that some such experience may cause a festering spot in the unconscious mind that must be dealt with by analysis. Fortunately, we tend to take the shocks in our stride and the wounds heal quickly. Children, especially, have remarkable recuperative powers.

With what may be a somewhat unfortunate over exposure to limited psychological information, we will want to guard carefully against becoming obsessed with the recollection of some childhood shock. A morbid preoccupation with the past may well result in the very thing occurring that we want to avoid. Actually, present or future facts may be far more significant in determining behavior. Personally, except with extreme and chronic cases, I prefer the use of synthesis-rather than analysis. In synthesis, the whole is considered — the present, the future, as well as the past. For example, the failure to find a satisfying expression and fulfillment of personality can produce intense frustration and the observable illness may be only an outward symptom of that frustration. Unless personal fulfillment can be achieved, analysis may do little to help. It might bring a temporary improvement, but the patient will inevitably relapse.

If a person has reached a place in life where his personality potential is inhibited, explosive energy which must find an outlet somewhere is being built up. Functional disease is such an outlet ("functional" refers to complaints which do not have a primary physical origin or cause).

To illustrate: The unconscious mind recalls an illness in childhood that resulted in immediate concentration of love and attention from others. Being in the spotlight — getting special concessions and considerations — was pleasant. Consequently in later life the unconscious mind may tend to regress to an early illness experience as a form of escape from a present failure or frustration. You see, our unconscious mind lies far below our conscious reach, but it can be influenced by unconsciously producing new and creative impressions. Through positive affirmation this new data will begin to influence the conscious process.

Unfortunately, the presence of regressive factors in a nervous breakdown is often conducive to guilt feelings. The patient feels badly because he can't "control himself." This feeling may be accentuated by ill-advised relatives who tell the patient to "take a grip on himself," usually adding that unless he does, he will "lose his mind." This attitude is completely unreasonable and unfair. While it is true that certain of the factors involved may be controllable, the same thing can be said of a broken leg. Usually, supreme acts of will are about as effective in curing a breakdown as they would be in curing a fracture.

The first step in any cure is to secure competent medical help. A nervous breakdown won't just disappear in time. Even if the symptoms were to ease without treatment, the onset of the disorder was evidence that something was seriously wrong underneath. Failure to act immediately may lengthen the duration of the illness later and perhaps make it chronic.

When the intensity of the nervous and mental disturbance requires it, the medical doctor may prescribe shock therapy. This holds unnecessary terrors for people. It is not painful, or dangerous. I have seen patients who have been completely incapacitated restored to health through this method in a relatively short time.

Shock treatment may be administered by means of insulin, chemicals or electricity. It is a controlled convulsion, during which the patient is anesthetized. Why it works and what it does is somewhat of a mystery. The important thing is that it does frequently make people better. After a treatment has been completed, there is generally a period of mental confusion, and temporary loss of memory. This is unpleasant but does not last long.

Then again, following careful diagnosis the doctor will prescribe certain drugs, perhaps antidepressants or tranquilizers. Unfortunately many people are reluctant to accept this help, because they feel that such help is a "crutch." Ridiculous! No one should feel badly about receiving assistance when it is needed and is prescribed.

Another vital aspect of therapy is "organized" or "scheduled" activity. A change of pace, new surroundings, varied activities, all help to redirect habit patterns into wholesome channels. Above all, avoid over concern, worry and impatience — these drain away nervous energy badly needed in the healing process.

From the psychological angle, one of the most necessary things is to "talk out" your life experience with a qualified person. Be willing to freely discuss any and all problems without a sense of shame — remember, we all have problems. Scratch beneath the surface and we are all pretty much the same. The important thing is to get help regardless of what is involved.

Beware of guilt. It is a potent crippler. Don't make the mistake of thinking that you can get away with a violation of your own conscience. Externally you may be unaware of any feeling of wrongdoing, but deep down, you may be torn apart. You cannot hope for recovery until you restore inward peace by doing what you know is right.

This not only applies to the abandoning of wrong action. It also means surrender to what is right. If we are not fulfilling our God-given obligations, the guilt can be as intense as if we are doing something immoral.

Indecision is also a robber of nervous energy. Here I am not referring to indecision between right and wrong, but between courses of action that may be neither right nor wrong — that is, those in which moral considerations are not primary. The only thing to do here is to think through the whole matter squarely and honestly with the help and guidance of God and then to make the best decision possible in the circumstances. Then, unless new factors arise or error in judgment becomes evident, stick to this decision and rest in it. To vacillate back and forth between decisions for no good reason but plain indecisiveness will cause trouble.

Prayer can be most helpful in the case of a nervous breakdown, provided the goals are right. Just merely praying to get better may not be effective. Of course, God always reserves the right to take any sovereign action He wishes. He can make us better in the flicker of an eyelid, but this is not likely, because He has allowed this infirmity to come about for a purpose. The quickest way to recover through prayer, therefore, is to ask God's help and guidance in fulfilling those purposes, whatever they are. This may be to put right something wrong with the body, or perhaps to make necessary repairs to the mental and spiritual life. God is more anxious to make us well than we are to be made well. Most likely He is just waiting for us to straighten out so that He can have a chance to work.

The best kind of prayer for a person with a nervous disorder is just light conversation: talking and sharing with God every fleeting thing that comes to the mind whether religious or not. This unburdens the mind on the one hand, and on the other, gives a sense of the Presence of God, which is the best reassuring thing in the world.

I have often heard it said that the surrendered Christian could never have a nervous breakdown because God wouldn't let it happen. There are two things wrong with this. "Surrender" is a matter of degree. God reveals greater areas of devotion to Him and His kingdom as we go along. Even if we are as totally dedicated as we can be at a certain stage of knowledge and experience, there is always a long way to go. Usually, the kind of person who makes such a sweeping statement as this is revealing a pride of Phariseeism about himself which is far from total commitment.

Secondly, such a statement assumes far too much insight into the mind and will of God. The fact is that for purposes best known to Himself, He permits breakdowns to occur in the most devoted of people.

All of us experience psychological tensions. None of us should consider ourselves immune, a change in hormone secretion, a sudden shock, an irritation in the unconscious, some bodily malfunction or illness could bring us low. There are perhaps a hundred factors we know nothing about which could render us useless and helpless.

But I do know that if one is finding for himself the good life, the chance of these factors triggering a breakdown will be extremely remote. The problems, conscious and unconscious, will still be there, but they will generally appear minute in the light of the satisfying life.

The Secret of the Satisfied Personality

2.2.155

9

The Secret of the Satisfied Personality

The body has its own built-in mechanism for healing, placed there by God Himself. All we can do (and that includes the physician and the psychologist) is to stimulate or aid those processes. *External* factors alone cannot heal.

We have already considered the problem of the nervous breakdown, a specialized area in the general subject of bodily healing. It was discussed separately because it is a major concern in clinical psychology. Because of the nature of the nervous breakdown, it is especially subject to the psychological and spiritual approach. However, much can be done about the general problem of bodily healing, as well.

Just how much bodily disease or malfunction can be cured through mental processes is hard to say. Some say that all physical ills are mental in origin and therefore can be put right by proper mental attitudes. The question is rather academic at this stage of medical knowledge, because now we experience both physical and mental factors in operation. Perhaps one day these mysterious factors will be resolved into one common underlying principle, but that is not likely to occur in our lifetime.

There is no need to look upon the physical and spiritual as being mutually exclusive anyway. They are different, but often mutually complementary methods of bringing about healing.

Lincoln Christian College

The physician is skilled in aiding these inner processes by physical means. He can tell by the symptoms of the illness just what the healing mechanism is up against. He also knows certain drugs or foods which can help. In some cases surgery is indicated as a means of eliminating the malfunction. It can be agreed that without this medical help, the patient might get better anyhow. This is quite possible. It is also possible that he would die without qualified medical attention.

This inner mechanism of natural healing is limited. Sometimes the factors of disease it has to fight prove too much for it. In that case the body dies. At other times the healing and disease forces are somewhat equal, then the result is permanent invalidism. If the healing process is predominant, the patient gets better. It is obvious, therefore, that the external aid given by the physician or medical science may be all that is required to tip the scales in favor of healing.

There are those who object to physical aids to healing as being something of a "crutch" or "unnatural," but so are cooked food, clothes, automobiles, elevators and a thousand other amenities of living. This does not make them wrong or undesirable. The Bible says that every good and perfect gift comes from above, so we should accept medical science as a gift from God and use it accordingly. Like most of God's gifts, medicine has to come to us through human channels and therefore is subject to human frailty and error, but it comes from God nevertheless. Would we deny a gift as coming from a friend if it were somewhat marred in the process of delivery?

Who could estimate the total good to mankind that has come through the practice of medicine? In our own time we need to be especially grateful to God for medical science. Terrible diseases have been eliminated. Wonder drugs have worked miracles. Surgery is doing the seemingly impossible. As a result, man's life is longer and freer from illness than ever before. In this he has found a new freedom to realize himself and be the person God wants him to be.

The psychologist approaches the matter of health from the aspect of the mind, but without any feeling whatever that he has all the answers. Obviously it doesn't make much sense to cure even a psychic symptom if it is caused by a physical disorder. Many malfunctions do have serious psychic symptoms, especially those affecting the brain, such as brain tumors. Indeed, at first sight, it is difficult to distinguish a brain tumor dysfunction from a nervous breakdown. Yet here an undue delay in surgery could be fatal.

On the other hand, it may be equally fruitless to treat a functional disease with medicine alone. In a previous chapter it was explained that a functional disease is one whose cause lies in the unconscious mind rather than in physical factors. The unconscious mind is simply the sum total of all a person's past experiences which are never really forgotten. It is called "unconscious" because the person is no longer aware of these experiences, neither can he recall them. There are, of course, experiences in the past which we can recall. These are "foreconscious."

Most of the experiences of the unconscious never give any trouble, especially if they were not emotionally tinged, but those with strong emotional content, including fears, wishes, drives or frustrated ego cravings, remain lively and may influence the person's health in most remarkable and tragic ways.

A famous case from World War I is a good illustration. A man on the western front was besieged by fear, which is quite understandable. All his instincts made him want to turn and run to a safe place behind the lines, but he knew he couldn't do that. Unfortunately, instead of recognizing his fear as normal, he was shocked and disgusted with himself and repressed the fear. One day a mortar shell landed near by and threw him into unconsciousness. When he came to, he was blind. After he was examined at a base hospital, it was found that his eyes had suffered no physical injury. Psychiatric inquiry revealed that his blindness was functional. It was a trick of his unconscious mind to solve his problem of removal from the front without being a coward.

Not all cases are as neat as this, by any means. The causes may be enormously complicated. The chief culprit appears to be ego frustration: the failure to find a satisfying life or the loss of a sense of achievement through drift or adverse circumstances. Sickness can then be the personality's solution. When sick, a person is no longer expected to achieve. He has an alibi for his failure, which eases the personality distress. Also sickness brings attention, which is always gratifying to the ego drive.

For these reasons some people deliberately induce illness into themselves. We call them "hypochondriacs." These are the unhappy people who have fled from the battles of living. It is most difficult to help them because they want to stay the way they are.

However, most people who suffer from psychophysical complaints are not cowards. They have simply been unfortunate enough to become the victims of their own unconscious minds. It is as easy to have this happen as it is to get an infection or develop appendicitis.

No one entirely avoids functional troubles. We may not develop functional blindness, paralysis, colitis, aphasia and such like, but our complaints may be backaches, indigestion, headaches and a hundred-and-one troubles which are not likely to kill us, but can make life pretty miserable. They may have physical causes, too, but can be irritated and prolonged if the unconscious mind should use them as a false personality satisfaction.

Physical illness can readily be induced by suggestion. This is also true of death. The Australian aborigine witchdoctor can point the sacred bone at an erring tribesman and that's it. The victim slinks away and dies.

When I was at the university, I went to a doctor for an eye checkup. He prescribed glasses, but I couldn't afford them. Immediately I began to suffer headaches, which I assumed were due to eyestrain. At length a friend persuaded me to go and see a qualified eye specialist. His verdict was that there was nothing wrong with my eyes and that I certainly did not need glasses. Just as suddenly, the headaches vanished. I had been the victim of autosuggestion. The facility with which this occurred was a real eye-opener. Apparently this kind of thing happens with the greatest of ease.

In the same way symptoms may also be removed by suggestion. Notice how the prestige of the specialist provided power enough through suggestion to remove my headaches.

Hypnosis is a special case of suggestion. The hypnotist puts his patient into a trance-like state when he can induce either symptoms or the removal of them in the unconscious mind.

At first sight it looks as if hypnosis is an ideal form of healing. It might be if the removal of symptoms is all that is required, but symptoms are not necessarily undesirable. They are nature's way of warning that there is something wrong with the organism. When the inner trouble is put right, the symptoms will disappear. To cure symptoms without dealing with the basic disorder is like a man shooting out the warning light on a level crossing where his car is stalled!

Hypnosis deals with symptoms and therefore its misuse could become dangerous. By its nature it does not always get at the heart of the trouble.

This does not mean that hypnosis is not useful. As a tool in the hands of a qualified psychologist it may be helpful in getting at the truth about obstinate repressions. It also has been found useful in alleviating or removing pain in childbirth, dentistry and some surgical operations. Here, of course, there is no worry about covering up the nature of the basic cause. It cannot be too strongly emphasized that no one should allow himself to be hynotized for amusement, and never by anyone but a qualified physician or psychologist.

Spiritual healing, faith healing, or healing through religious methods are not essentially different from medical science or psychology. The aim is identical: to stimulate the natural, God-given processes of healing within the person.

Sometimes spiritual healing occurs with startling directness. The sick person prays, or someone prays for him, and healing is instantaneous. There are many cases of this in the Bible, and it still occurs, even though it is somewhat rare. In most instances, recovery is gradual.

Many abortive attempts have been made to determine the exact conditions under which God will grant instantaneous healing. The idea is to set up a religious push-button system which will make healing automatic. This is as futile as any other attempt to reduce God to a system. He acts when He wants to and how He wants to. One person may be healed and under identical circumstances another may die. Think of the few people Christ healed in His lifetime in comparison with those who gained no relief.

Neither will God be bound by any particular method. In New Testament days there was no uniformity. Healing could be by the spoken word alone, by prayer, by touch, by anointing with oil — in the patient's presence or in his absence. Sometimes it was associated with faith, supplication, or spiritual attitudes on the sick person's part, but sometimes not. There just isn't any fixed pattern.

The same is true about the agent for healing. Healing could be accomplished by Christ or a disciple or even in the absence of any human intermediary.

There can be no doubt but that God would like to see all sickness eliminated, but it is also obvious that He sometimes refrains from healing because He is accomplishing something more important in the long run, and the healing would interfere with this. There are a number of cases in the New Testament where healing did not occur even though there was such an outbreak of miracles in those days.

The Bible makes it clear that all human suffering has *its origin* in human sin, but this is in a corporate sense. Thus it does not follow that a righteous, God-fearing life will guarantee good health or freedom from trouble, although it will predispose toward this. We often get caught up in the results of the sinning of others when we are blameless ourselves. In any case, there is no way of escaping the dire results of the sins of the human race of long ago. The stream of evil was started in the infancy of the race, and since then it has swept the good and the bad along with it.

Generally speaking, there is no connection between unpleasant events and individual acts of righteousness or sin. That is, if I develop appendicitis, it would be pointless of me to assume that God is punishing me for some wrong act. Or, if I get a raise, it would be wrong for me to interpret this as a God-given reward for going to the prayer meeting.

Christ was once asked whether a man's blindness was due to his own sin or his parents' (John 9:2). He quickly showed that it was not caused by either. In the Sermon on the Mount, He taught the impartiality of God, who sends His sunshine and rain upon the just and the unjust (Matthew 5:45). Obviously, this is the only way God could act if righteousness is to be its own reward. If God were to place a fence around the good and the spiritual to protect them from material evil, Christianity would quickly become a substitute for casualty insurance.

Although we can assume that, in general, God doesn't deal out arbitrary physical punishment, this does not mean that He is incapable of doing so. In the New Testament, Ananias and

Sapphira were struck with death for lying (Acts 5:1-10), and Elymas was afflicted with blindness for opposing the Gospel (Acts 13:11). Usually in cases like this, more than the individual is involved. God has to act to protect His own purposes and plans. Whenever we attempt to trifle with God, we do so at our own peril. He is not petty or vindictive, but the attitude of Christ toward the Pharisees shows that He can be extremely severe, especially when others are hurt by sin.

Of course, all of us, through human frailty, get caught up in sin, but what has been said in the previous paragraph does not entail any insecurity for us. God is loving and understanding to those whose hearts are right in spite of their weakness. Also, there is always complete protection in His forgiveness. Whenever we ask for that forgiveness, He wipes the slate completely clean.

This does not take into account the cause-and-effect process which is a different matter altogether since it is part of natural law and does not involve divine intervention. If I drink to excess, I may get cirrhosis of the liver; if I drive too fast, I may have an accident; if I waste my substance, I may finish up in poverty. God seldom intervenes to prevent these natural consequences.

At first sight, this Biblical view of the present inevitability of human suffering and the impartiality of God is rather frightening. It seems to place us at the mercy of forces which are beyond us, but this is not really so. God also gives His guidance. As long as we are surrendered to His will, He will make sure that no *unnecessary* ills befall us. Everything for the Christian remains under God's control. Troubles will still come, but our welfare in the long run is always guaranteed.

In summary of this question of sickness and the will of God, it may be said that when sickness strikes, it could be because the patient has placed himself outside of God's guidance and thus has come to grief, or because God has allowed the onset for purposes known only to Himself. Even in the latter case, it does not mean God is unwilling to heal. It is the privilege of everyone to go to God in prayer for help at any time.

The question immediately arises: what conditions do we have to fulfill before God will heal? There is no simple answer to this because God is sovereign and will not be bound. But the Scriptures do seem to offer some specific guidance and suggest certain steps the Christian may take.

The most notable of these is faith. This is sadly misunderstood. It is certainly no mere intellectual assent to the existence of God or even of His power to heal. Neither does it mean believing that He is necessarily going to heal — this would be impertinence. Faith is the total commitment of the person to Him until he is completely at His disposal.

Catherine Marshall has reported that God did not begin to accede to her prayers for healing from TB until she told Him He could do what He wanted with her, even to permanent invalidism and death. At that moment of surrender, God started to work in a marvelous way.

Our trouble is often that we want God to intervene in only one localized area: our sickness. We want to keep the rest of our lives under our own control, but this is a practical impossibility. The "whole man" must be healed — faith places the total person in His hands.

Prayer is generally associated with healing. It simply means talking with God about the problem. Behind prayer should be the confidence that He is anxious to heal, if this is in our best interests. We insult Him when we act as if He is reluctant and needs to be persuaded. He is not deaf, so we do not need to shout our requests to the rooftops, and neither should we deluge Him with words, assuming that He will hear us for our much speaking (Matthew 6:7).

On the other hand, prayer for healing must not be perfunctory. When we casually and momentarily place the request before God, and then completely forget Him, we don't really believe in Him. We need to bathe ourselves in the sense of His presence and keep ourselves there.

An obvious question on the matter of spiritual healing is that of the professional faith healer, or the healing meeting. Now, God can heal through anyone and under any circumstance. We cannot deny that genuine cases of healing do occur through the faith healing medium, but they do appear to be rare. God seems to do most of His healing unostentatiously and privately.

Sufferers should be warned that a great deal of racketeering occurs in the name of faith healing. In the name of religion, human parasites prey upon the longings of suffering people. The law enforcement authorities do what they can, but the real answer lies with people themselves refusing to deal with these charlatans.

It is true that much of false faith healing appears convincing — blind people see, deaf people hear, lame people walk. However this can be merely the temporary effects of suggestion. Such "healings" usually promptly disappear once the impact of the meeting is over.

Sometimes these so-called "healings" are staged. The healer may arrange beforehand for perfectly well people to simulate illness and thus recover at his word.

One way in which we can usually distinguish the false from the genuine is in the atmosphere of the meeting. If it is deliberately worked up with shouting and yelling or other hypnotic devices, be on the elert. These are the trappings that generally accompany the operation of suggestion. It should be obvious that God does not need props to effect His miracles.

However, we must be careful in our judgments. Many sincere and devoted people are seeking to learn more about spiritual healing and do hold special meetings in which they pray for sufferers. With these you will find nothing of the bizarre or the extravagant. Neither will the use of medicine and psychology be disparaged. They recognize the recuperative powers that God has placed within and are anxious to use every genuine means to set them in motion.

The physical, the psychological and the spiritual are merely different aspects of the total personality. It has been necessary to look at each of these in some detail, but it should be remembered that such a division is always somewhat artificial. It is what happens to the total personality that counts.

We have seen throughout this book that the human personality is characterized by an unceasing drive for expression and fulfillment and that when this is realized a feeling of well-being, happiness and contentment results. It is when this is blocked or lags behind its potential that trouble and unhappiness begins.

Bodily illness plays a vital part in the struggle for fulfillment. In some cases it appears as a symptom of lack of fulfillment, or as a spurious fulfillment when normal channels are blocked or unused.

In the state of unfulfillment or frustration the personality, powered by its unsatisfied inner drive, is like a drowning man clutching at a straw. Normally, recognition is the mark of realization of the potential, but sometimes the hungry personality will bypass this and reach for the recognition without the attainment. Bodily illness offers an easy channel for this. When we are sick, our loved ones heap attention upon us. We become miniature kings or queens in our own right.

It follows that the frustrated personality is a breeding ground for bodily illness. In other words, if we want to remain healthy, we must make sure we are using our total potential at all times.

Now, even if a sickness is not caused by the frustrated personality, it may be perpetuated or irritated by it. In this way a simple ailment may refuse to respond to treatment and become chronic. Sometimes the ailment itself may get better only to be replaced by others in a weary succession. If a person becomes afflicted with such a succession of apparently unrelated sicknesses, it would be well for him to make a serious appraisal. It could be that he is just run down physically and therefore unable to resist the germ invasions. It also could be that his unconscious mind is beginning to form an unholy pattern of pseudo-satisfaction through attention-getting illness.

Unless we are giving full and satisfying expression to the needs of the personality, the work of the doctor, the psychologist or the minister will be seriously hindered. As we have seen in an earlier chapter, total commitment to God cannot occur without this kind of personality outreach. It is part of the significance of faith itself, and thus a vital factor in healing.

Now, just as the unsatisfied personality predisposes the body to illness, so also sickness can detract from personal fulfillment in a vicious kind of feedback. It is important, therefore, for an ailing person to take positive action about his troubles. No matter how desperate the complaint may be, there is no reason to give up hope. Medical science is constantly coming up with astounding new cures. Who knows what is around the next corner?

What if God should see fit not to intervene? Let's face it; this does constitute a serious limitation to personality expression, but it need not deter adequate fulfillment. All of us have obstacles of some description or another. The record of the past is full of people who accomplished marvelous things in spite of physical handicaps.

The cripple or the invalid has two possible courses of action. He may give up entirely and add a crippled personality to a crippled body, or he may seek for other means of fulfillment which can make life rich and satisfying.

Over and above all, we should be aware of the Christian teaching that important though the body is, it is only a temporary housing. Inside is the personality, the soul, the real man, and this is eternal. What we invest in this, nothing can take away. This kind of fulfillment is open to all, regardless of physical disability.

Breaking the Chains

10

Breaking the Chains

Human personality must be free. If ever its legitimate freedom of expression is blocked in any way, the result is extreme anguish.

Perhaps the most distressing of all the obstacles to freedom are those which come from the inside. To be chained by others is bad enough, but to be enmeshed in a slavery of our own making is galling indeed. Yet this is exactly what happens when we become the victims of habits, or what our forefathers aptly called "besetting sins."

The Bible uses a dramatic analogy for this kind of problem. It occurs in Paul's epistle to the Romans, chapter 7. In vivid imagery he cries, "Who shall deliver me from the body of this death?" Expositors have suggested that he is referring to a cruel practice of the Romans by which a murderer was chained face to face with his victim and the two thrown into a dungeon, the living destined to a horrible death in the arms of the decaying corpse.

Apparently at one time in his life the great apostle found himself chained to an evil like that. He would make up his mind not to act in this fashion again, yet when the temptation recurred, he would succumb. No matter how he tried, he could not break loose until he found his freedom through the Christian Gospel.

An appropriate illustration of this in modern times is the alcoholic. He hates himself for what he is doing to himself, his family and his future, yet he is seemingly powerless to resist. In spite of all his efforts he sees himself being dragged inexorably down to ruin and perhaps premature death.

Drug addiction and obsessive gambling are two more terrible forms of personality slavery in which the victim loses all respect for himself and the feelings of others. Life in such bondage becomes so impossible that many of these unhappy people take their own lives.

Although these are the habits that make the headlines because of the serious damage they do, there are many other chains that can make a person powerless to find the good life. These are more insidious than spectacular, but they also reap a dreadful harvest in terms of human misery.

Probably the most common of all is a bad temper. This has been referred to as a form of insanity, for under its influence a person loses all sense of reason and prudence. He may say things and do things that he would never dream of doing in his right mind. Moreover, he is quite capable of inflicting deep hurt even on his closest loved ones. When something triggers it, the outburst is on its way and it is as uncontrollable as a hurricane. The exploding force of anger can wear down a marriage until it breaks apart; it can make children's lives a misery and fill life with insecurity and unpleasantness.

Some people are creatures of moods. All of us, of course, have our emotional ups and downs. Most of this variation is caused by tiny differences in the secretions of the hormones from the endocrine glands into the blood stream. There are many, however, who habitually give way to these moods, inflicting gloom and depression on those around them. Many a child fearfully watches father's face in the morning for signs that he has gotten up "on the wrong side of the bed." These are the people who are not emotionally housebroken — an understandable weakness in childhood but pathetic in grown people.

Then there is the compulsive Casanova who must go on from conquest to conquest of the other sex. While the chase is on, the winning of the particular victim becomes the all-consuming goal of life, for which he may sacrifice everything. Then when the seduction is complete, the whole thing turns to ashes. While the victim is left to face heartbreak and loss of self-respect, the trifler goes on to newer conquests, and so the whole sorry process is repeated ad infinitum, ad nauseum. No man can become so sophisticated that he does not despise himself for living a life without integrity like this, but he may be powerless to break free.

In some lives this romantic obsession may strike only once, but then with appalling suddenness. A man may have been happily married for years, devoted to his family, with a spotless record behind him, and still become embroiled in some tawdry affair. He may see clearly where it is all leading and be torn apart by the havoc he is causing and yet be powerless to call a halt.

The gossip and the critic are also slaves. Compelled to belittle the achievements of others, they cannot hear a piece of unsavory information even about their friends without passing it on. Their range of vision is limited to the apprehension of faults and frailties. They are sour and unhappy people because they are imprisoned in a world of evil.

Pathological lying is another case in point. Here the victim is incapable of telling the plain truth. Everything has to be colored, embellished and distorted. It may start harmlessly enough but in time it becomes a compulsion.

In a few cases these obsessions are symptoms of serious mental disease, but only rarely. As a rule, they are faults of the personality with the remedy within the reach of almost everyone.

The fact that these traits of behavior can assume such enormous power is significant. It is obvious that underneath there is some hidden drive. It also follows that unless this drive is redirected, trying to break free will be impossible.

The drive that causes all this trouble is nothing new. It is the same ego craving for fulfillment that we have discussed throughout this book. Only here, denied its normal expression, it has diverted itself into undesirable channels.

In the case of the alcoholic, the evidence is plain in the antics of the drunkard. When intoxicated, a man's personality may undergo a complete change. The self-conscious person stands on a table and sings a song. Alcohol gives a spurious sense of fulfillment, a counterfeit. It is true that the alcohol may set up physical cravings, but this is not the real problem. It is both psychological and spiritual. The alcoholic is a victim of his own nature. Unless he can change the course of this drive, all the medical help in the world would be doomed to failure.

Drug addiction is much more serious because of the chemical affinity set up by the physical organism. However, it is still powered by the same drive, as is proved by the fact that addicts attempting to kick the habit feel an overpowering need for the drug at times of personal failure or rejection by others, that is, failure to find normal fulfillment.

Gambling appears to be an attempt at aggrandizement by tangling with the odds of fate or some such mysterious force. When the gambler wins, he feels he has achieved a superhuman victory. Winning is compensation for the failings and boredom of living.

Bad temper is a primitive and futile attempt to overpower some person who has given us a bloody-nosed ego. The injury may be physical or mental, but it adds up to the same thing. Fulfillment along the lines desired has been denied. Instead of handling the problem in a positive and rational manner, we attempt to overwhelm the opponent by an outburst of emotion. This seldom works, and even if it does happen to succeed, we are left with the frustration of knowing that we have cheated at the game.

Moodiness and depression are often attention-getting devices. Of course, if the problem is pronounced, psychiatric help is indicated, but moods are quite common in normal people. It is a juvenile attempt by the mind to gain that spotlight denied because of personal failure to achieve.

Some discussion of the problem of the person who flirts has been offered already. It has been seen that he is not an over-sexed person. He is an insecure person trying desperately to prove himself by personal physical conquest. It never works, although it is heady wine while it lasts, but at the bottom of the glass there are the dregs: disillusionment.

The analysis of gossip and criticism is also comparatively easy. Personality stature between people is relative. We can either become tall by positive growth, or we can appear tall by pushing the other person down. When we belittle someone else we are trying, in an infantile way, to cut him down so we will feel bigger. It is an evil process, not only because it may hurt someone else, but also because it siphons off the incentive to positive achievement on our part.

The cause behind lying is the same. Instead of accomplishing worthwhile things himself, the liar resorts to fiction. In real life he is a failure. In his stories, he is important, a success.

In every case, the basic cure must inevitably be the same: to find a positively satisfying life by all-round personal fulfillment. If the energies of the personality are being used up in this way, there will be none left to feed the habits; they will lose their power, wither and die.

A victim will often deny that this is the problem, and at first sight he may seem to be right. He may be active, prosperous and important, but this is not necessarily enough. Fulfillment is relative to his ability at any particular stage in his life. Unless he is realizing his maximum potential, his surplus energy will be as dangerous as leaving spilled gasoline lying around.

This chapter opened with a reference to the experience of the Apostle Paul and his victory through the Christian Gospel. Paul allied himself to the divine Presence within, which gave him a purpose and goal in living. All his energies were concentrated on his new God-given crusade to bring the message of Christ to the ancient world. With Paul there was never any surplus. When religious people remain slaves to personality evils, they are obviously lacking in the kind of commitment that characterized the great apostle.

Paul also laid claim to another function of the indwelling Presence. He experienced a progressive integration with God, who permeated the life and drove out the undesirable things. This is going a step further in the use of personality power: the harnessing of the personality of God to the purpose of breaking the chains.

To work, this must be more than a mere theoretical concept. The divine presence must be realized in day-by-day experience. It must be *felt*.

This goes further than faith. Faith knows He is there. Experience takes it from there and goes out to find Him. It is fired by imagination, not the imagination of fiction but the imagination of the scientist who figures a Pluto is there in orbit, and looks for it in his telescope until he finds it. This consciousness of God may be weak at first, but it will grow with practice. Ultimately, the sense of the Presence is so real that the practice of evil habits becomes impossible. In such an experience the human personality finds its greatest fulfillment.

The conquering of an evil habit requires walking a fine line. It necessitates a recognition of defeat and a concern about it, without being obsessed with it. The victim who worries constantly about his chains only binds them more tightly. Any idea, good or evil, grows by attention to it. The trick is to shift the attention away from the evil thing and let it starve. This shifting also includes prayer. In the Scriptures we are urged to reject our sins and to ask forgiveness for them, but we are not asked to concentrate on them in prayer. This would only entangle us further.

In a remarkable passage Paul writes (Philippians 4:8) ". . . . whatsoever things are true, whatsoever things are honest, whatsoever things are just, whatsoever things are pure, whatsoever things are lovely, whatsoever things are of good report . . . think on these things." This is excellent advice. While we are filled with the ideas of the lovely and the good, there is no mental attention left to feed the evil. This ties in well with what was said above about the divine Presence. If we allow ourselves to be captured with the magnetism of His personality, evil will not only wither, it will be burned up.

So far, we have been concerned with long-range solutions, but every victim of personality evil knows that he needs practical help meanwhile, otherwise he may become discouraged and abandon himself to defeat.

The alcoholic may be helped a great deal by his doctor with whom he should have a frank and close association. Sometimes a drug like "Antabuse" will help, but results from this quarter haven't been too heartening. Alcoholics Anonymous has been infinitely more successful. This admirable organization uses many devices, but the most useful is person-to-person contact. When the alcoholic feels the temptation coming, he always has a person to whom he can telephone for help: another alcoholic. Together they can beat the thing down. Also in A.A. the alcoholic takes on a new importance. He is not only a victim to be helped, but he has a responsibility to help someone else. He becomes useful, wanted. His personality drive is harnessed for the cure.

The drug addict is in much greater peril. Usually he has to be hospitalized and be forced to endure the agonies of withdrawal. Unless the treatment is given on his own initiative, his will is quite inadequate to see him through. Once the habit has been "kicked," he needs person-to-person help, either through trusted friends and loved ones or through such movements as Narcotics Anonymous.

The gambling evil is purely within the mind, so medicine doesn't help here, but the A.A. method is relevant. For this reason, we also have Gamblers Anonymous. However, this movement is not widespread enough to be of much help, largely because the incidence of compulsive gamblers is much smaller than that of alcoholism. Still any kind of person-to-person check will do. As with the alcoholic and the drug addict, the obsessive gambler needs to realize that his abstinence must be total. There can be no concessions, no exceptions.

The elimination of uncontrolled rage largely depends on alertness to possible temptation. Usually, there are readily identifiable provocations which trigger the anger. These should be carefully noted and a watch kept that they do not catch the victim napping. It helps also to admit the failures, with apologies to those who have been hurt.

In the cases of "moods," we have more warning. There is a general feeling of malaise, out of which the self-pity and irritability grows. When the mood sets in, it may be driven away by making an effort to become absorbed in some interesting activity. The victim won't want to do this. He will be blocked by heavy inertia, but if he has the courage and the drive to win, he will break through this barrier regardless of feelings.

Of course, the "Casanova" needs to do something about his moral problem, and this goes deeper than the sexual immorality. When a man thinks so little of the welfare of another person that he will wilfully trifle with her affections and even destroy her, he is about as close to what is meant by a lost soul as it is possible to get. A man without compassion is no man at all.

If he really is concerned about breaking the habit, such a man will be so much on the alert that he will not allow himself to get involved — he will recognize that platonic friendships are not for him.

The best device the compulsive critic can use is to make a nightly (before retiring) check on the conversations of the day, asking God's forgiveness for failures. It also helps to use the temptation to belittle as an occasion for praise instead.

As for the liar, he usually becomes aware of his defeat as the conversation proceeds. By then he feels it is too late to do anything about it, and that he might as well be killed for a sheep as a lamb. However, this is the point where he can break the habit by admitting the prevarication. This can be done as a joke by saying, "And that makes me the world's greatest liar," or something to that effect.

Eloquent in Speech

11

Eloquent in Speech

Speech is the messenger of the personality. It enables one to grow through outreach, to cleanse pent-up emotions, to win goals in the world of men, to transport inner riches for the use of living people and to be the vehicle of the love and message of God to His earthly creatures.

God places enormous importance on speech. He even calls His Son — the Word of God. In Jesus He expresses the secrets of His own nature in a living human and divine being so that in His life and words people can recognize the Almighty. He calls the Bible, the Word of God, because it is the direct revelation of His message to men. He even calls preaching the Gospel, the Word of God because He uses it to touch people so that they may see His truth.

The term, The Word, comes from Greek thought. The Greeks thought in terms of a stream of ideas emanating from God and striking human minds to be reflected as human knowledge. In this sense our speech is a transmission from God or from the devil. We become like microwave pick-up stations receiving messages and sending them on to others.

Radio transmission depends on two major processes. First, there is the carrier wave, the electro-magnetic stream, the power and direction of which determines the penetration of the broadcast. Superimposed upon this are the electrical impulses generated by the microphone and which modify the carrier. This determines the message of the broadcast.

The transmission of ideas through speech is somewhat similar. The carrier is the power of the personality. The content is determined by the language used. An inadequate personality will nullify even the most beautiful or the most searching language. Halting or inadequate words and delivery will mar the message. There is no reason why we can't work on both of these factors at the same time.

In the previous pages it has been shown that the development of personality power is a matter of keeping all the inner abilities challenged and extended. It means harnessing the relentless ego drive until it finds its satisfaction in satisfying activity. It means allowing God to permeate every corner of the being so that He can stimulate our God-given powers into action and fulfillment.

Such realization is relative. What satisfied the ego yesterday is no longer adequate today. The elasticity of the personality has caused an increased capacity which requires even greater effort.

The attention which speech, public or private, demands is directly proportionate to personality tension in the speaker. It is not the negative tension of anxiety and stress, but the positive tension of a personality that is alert, eager and expectant. This can only come about when we are living a totally satisfying life all the time. We cannot simulate it or cork it up for a particular occasion. It has to be there already — solid, powerful, convincing. Without this background, even the most diligent attention to the techniques of speech, proves worse than useless. The effect on the listener is that of something hollow, artificial or academic.

Failure or inadequacy in communication is a common enemy to human unhappiness for it leaves the personality imprisoned. It is terribly frustrating to the ego which longs for the fulfillment of being understood and recognized by others. Curiously enough, the ego is its own greatest barrier to this longed-for satisfaction. Its very anxiety to succeed often sets up inhibitions which doom all efforts to failure. Especially in speech are we prone to self-consciousness and this can cloud the mind, block the memory and garble the words.

Trying hard to overcome this problem is as bad as struggling with the water when you fall in and can't swim. This is the law of reversed effort: what you try too hard not to do, you finish up doing. When you struggle not to be self-conscious, you focus the mind on the problem and draw its energy into the sore spot rather than the job in hand. It is absolutely essential to shift the focus of the attention off one's self, for then the self-consciousness will die for sheer lack of energy intake.

This was a serious problem for me. When I was young, I desperately wanted to succeed and win approval. The talks I prepared for Christian Endeavor were forged out in blood, sweat and tears. No matter how carefully I prepared, when I stood to my feet, self-consciousness rose like a flood. Several times I completely forgot everything I planned to say and I had to sit down in embarrassment. Even when things weren't quite as bad as this, my stammering efforts were pitiful.

One night at a Salvation Army open-air meeting, my young heart became filled with compassion when I saw some pathetic broken creatures listening nearby. Something made me get into that ring and tell them in a few short sharp words what God meant to me and what I felt He could do for them. I had forgotten about myself entirely and hadn't given a thought to success or failure. As a result, there was no self-consciousness and the message was fluent and clear. From that moment I never looked back. Whenever I had anything to say, either in public or private, I let myself become obsessed with the needs of the listeners and the importance of my message.

Attention to the listener and to the message not only helps

in eliminating self-consciousness but also neutralizes the ego struggle between the speaker and the listener. If it is obvious to the listener that the speaker is focused on himself, he will rebel. When people speak to us in public or private we like to feel that they are interested in us. This gives us the ego satisfaction of feeling important and we become open to the ideas of the speaker.

After all, isn't this the Christian way? Instead of seeking things for ourselves we should be devoted to God and others. In seeking the interests of others we never lose, for it brings greater satisfaction in the long run.

This principle properly applied can save us from many errors and especially from that cardinal sin of the human voice: being a bore.

Others become bored when we talk about things in which they have no interest. We may be so obsessed with our own interests that we simply inflict them on others. If we haven't anything to say of interest to others, we had better be quiet.

In conversation, this means slanting what is said to the interests of the listener. It means having the Christian grace to study his reactions carefully so that we will know when he is bored and immediately switch our topic of discussion.

Now at times we do have something to say in which the listener is not *naturally* interested. For example, ministers often experience this problem. Since our message is from God, we cannot be silent, yet we must still respect the listener's personality. The answer is to create interest, to slant the message so that it will touch him on points that are important to him.

Long-windedness is a serious fault. It can become an obsession. Some people talk in an endless stream without allowing the listener any time to answer. This is a tip-off of an unsatisfied personality which is desperately trying to find a substitute satisfaction in sheer talk, regardless of what it does to others. With most of us, it may not be serious, but whenever we bore another person it does mean that we have not been sensitive enough to him to know when to stop.

Rambling is also a speech perversion and equally torturing to those who listen. Because of word association as we talk on a particular subject, all kinds of interesting branches will automatically suggest themselves. If we have no regard for the feelings of others, we will just follow these in our talk, but if we are really bent on pleasing and helping others we will discipline ourselves to keep to the point.

Incidentally, this is the key to a good public address. There should be one general theme, one specific point we want to put over. We may illustrate this, we may give ramifications of it, but we should never be sidetracked from the fixed goal. At every point the audience should have no difficulty following us.

Christian love for the listener will also prevent us from using the speech or conversation to show off superior knowledge which may be beyond the comprehension of the listener. As a rule, what we cannot put into simple language we do not really understand ourselves! Being pedantic is stupid. It is a childish way of grasping at ego satisfaction, but it is quite common. We truly achieve when we grasp the profound and make it understandable.

The unnecessary use of big words is also childish. The excuse is sometimes given that these obscure, lumbering giants are necessary to give the finer shades of meaning, but how can the listener detect such finesse when he doesn't even know what the words mean? The simpler the vocabulary, the better.

Facility with speech is obviously dependent on knowledge of the language. Schools have engineered the education program so that every adult should have mastered the English language in both vocabulary and grammar, but many slip through the net. If there is any lack here, we have an urgent responsibility to make up for the lack. The remedy is not hard to obtain. Almost every city has extension courses and there are numerous correspondence offerings.

Much more than mere language mechanics is needed however. Speeches, conversation, books and articles are full of allusion to literature, history and religion. Much of this can be unintelligible unless we read widely and constantly.

Some people, due to physical or psychological defects, are unfortunate enough to have speech handicaps. In these cases experts should be consulted. It is marvelous what modern medical science can do.

Stuttering is one of these painful defects. The nature of this is not fully known, but psychological factors apparently play a major part. For instance, it is significant that stammering often occurs in children who have over-talkative mothers. The child is driven by his ego to express himself in speech but finds it difficult to get in a word edgewise. When he does start to say something he is interrupted. This makes him fearful that the same will occur the next time. There is psychological hesitancy and the result is a stammer.

The cure of stammering is a matter for specialists — and this affliction can be cured. The victim can help himself a great deal by cultivating a confident psychological atmosphere in himself.

It is worthwhile noticing in passing that Demosthenes of ancient Greece, reputed to be the greatest orator who ever lived, started life as a stutterer. He became obsessed with the need to persuade his countrymen to stand up against the threat of Philip of Macedon. So, to proclaim this message, he practiced speech control by manipulating pebbles in his mouth. He developed lung power by running up hills and increased volume by practicing his speeches against the roar of the waves. His methods may not have been scientific, but his drive and perseverance more than made up for that.

Eloquent in Speech

Much is being said today in the field of personal counseling about "failure to communicate." This is especially true in marriage problems. It does not mean that the people involved are deaf and dumb nor that they are illiterate. The problem is either that they do not talk at all about their heartaches or that when they do talk they are misunderstood.

Many a wife feels helpless and rejected because her husband will not talk over his problems. He may flatly deny that he (or they) has any difficulties or he may simply evade talking about them. His reticence may be due to pride. Unfortunately, some men consider problems to be the result of personal failure and thus painful to the ego — or there may be a fear of rejection or ridicule.

The wife may have been responsible for this state of affairs. Perhaps he did once mention to her his troubles with his boss but instead of sympathy and understanding got the response: "What sort of mouse are you that you don't stand up to him?"

To a sensitive man, that is all it takes.

These same problems are shared by both men and women.

Needless to say, women have the same problems with men. The trouble is that our egos force us into all kind of disguises. We can't admit that we feel we are failures, so we talk around the problems or keep silent, desperately hoping that our partners will sense the real trouble and say something reassuring and encouraging. When they don't, we turn on them in anger and frustration.

In marriage we have a great responsibility to learn the language of our partners — and that doesn't mean English! Every person has a way of saying things or of not saying things which follow a definite emotional pattern. The words are unimportant. We must reach beyond the words and find out what the soul is trying to say. The secret of marital happiness is to understand and then say and do the things that are necessary for the welfare and happiness of the other person.

It is also important to learn the language of our children. Your teenage boy is facing an important social event and says:

"I hope my old jalopy will last out the evening. It doesn't sound too good."

If you say: "You have nothing to worry about. I checked that ignition myself only yesterday," you will have misunderstood his language.

What he really was trying to say was: "Dad, I want to look real good tonight, so I'd like to borrow your new car."

It is useless for you to argue: "Why doesn't he come right out and say that?"

Maybe that is not his language. Perhaps he is protecting himself from the ego suffering of a possible refusal. It could be that he wanted the thrill of your showing confidence in him by offering him the car.

Pride in family life is very sad. What a different world it would be if we could just eat "humble pie" and make a clean breast of our troubles, our hopes, our fears and our frustrations! We are so terribly ashamed to let down our hair and admit that we're human after all. It is true that this is difficult for the ego to take, but the road to the heights of achievement often lies through the valley of humility.

When you come to think of it, it is amazing what a few words can do. They can lift us up to the heights of joy or plunge us into the depths of gloom. All around us people are being affected by words. Day after day, words fall from our lips and determine the happiness or unhappiness of those for whom Christ lived and died.

It is fitting to quote what the Bible says about speech (James 3:2-5, *Amplified New Testament.*)

For we all often stumble and fall and offend in many things. And if any one does not offend in speech — never says the wrong things — he is a fully developed character and a perfect man, able to control his whole body and to curb his entire nature.

If we set bits in the horses' mouths to make them obey us, we can turn their whole bodies about.

Likewise look at the ships, though they are so great and are driven by rough winds, they are steered by a very small rudder whenever the impulse of the helmsman determines. Even so the tongue is a little member, and it can boast of great things. See how much wood or how great a forest a tiny spark can set ablaze!

Age Without Weariness

12

Age Without Weariness

The greatest killer of old age is not heart disease or cancer, but the loss of anything worthwhile living for. There are countless men who retire from busy, active lives in the prime of life. Their bodies are strong. Yet in retirement they wither and decay and often go down to an early grave.

This only happens, however, when they retire without anything absorbing enough to capture their imagination. Those who have something to live for gear their bodies and minds to continuing vigor and health.

The key is exactly the same as that to the other problems of human unhappiness discussed in this book: the craving of the personality for achievement and fulfillment.

It would appear as though our modern concept of old age brings to mind a body that is showing the wear and tear of the years, beset by fatigue and ailment. It is true that we can expect some disability because of age but the sunset years can still be the most useful and the most satisfying time in a person's life.

The Bible encourages this outlook. Moses was 80 years old when he was given the colossal task of delivering the nation of Israel from slavery. He didn't retire from this task until he was 120! God used many young men, too, but not just because they were young. Youth or age makes little difference to Him. He chooses a man for what he is in his inner-being.

There are some beautiful thoughts in Isaiah 40:29-31 which show how God works. They read as follows:

> He giveth power to the faint; and to them that have no might he increaseth strength.
>
> Even the youths shall faint and be weary, and the young men shall utterly fall:
>
> But they that wait upon the Lord shall renew their strength; they shall mount up with wings as eagles; they shall run, and not be weary; and they shall walk, and not faint.

Our whole attitude toward retirement and old age is going through a welcome change. Instead of thinking of it as a time when we are put out to pasture, we look upon it as the beginning of an entirely new career. Especially for those retired on a pension, it means the freedom to do something truly significant without the restriction of working merely to earn a living.

God has been good to us in our time. Because of the wonder of medicine and surgery, He not only has added years to our life expectancy, but He has also made it possible for these years to be healthy ones.

In many cases we can make our earthly span even longer and healthier by safeguarding the health we have. Good food, plenty of exercise, adequate rest, peace of mind: these are not modern by any means, but they are still vitally important. A frequent medical checkup can spot troubles before they become chronic.

When physical difficulties are detected, doctors today can achieve "wonders." Increasingly they are even replacing vital organs. At the time of this writing, Mississippi surgeons have taken out a diseased heart and replaced it with a good one.

It is true the patient did not survive long, but this is just the beginning!

We still have many dreadful diseases which disable and kill, but we are eliminating them one by one. No one can say that any disease is incurable any more. Although we may not have the answer at the moment, who knows what is just around the corner?

Before retirement a man finds challenge and satisfaction in his job, but then he looks forward to retirement, when he doesn't have to get up early in the morning, when he can fish at will or golf at leisure. At first, retirement appears as one long paradise, but gradually a sense of uneasiness creeps in. His inner potential starts to hunger for the satisfaction of striving against odds. Before long the frustration and misery become unbearable. He may finish up a hopeless drunk or a pathetic hypochondriac, seeking childish attention in real or imagined ills.

As the ego starves to death, it may drag down the body with it. The unconscious mind knows when life has lost significance. It will quickly break down the body to match it.

The misery of unfulfilled ego makes a person hard to live with. Recently, a woman came to see me, threatening to divorce her recently retired husband, yet they had been married for forty years. Her outburst was typical.

"He's become impossible. One moment he is criticizing everything I do, the next he is moody and silent. He's under my feet all the time. I just can't stand it any more."

The man had retired from a responsible position, now he had nothing. So he was encouraged to take a community service job. In no time at all, he was his old, genial, good natured self again.

Retirement has opened up a huge reservoir of manpower for Christian service. Our big twin problem in evangelism has been the lack of men and money. We are not even beginning to keep up with the world population increase, let alone win it for Christ, but here are tens of thousands of earnest people, many of them able to support themselves, just aching for something significant to do!

It used to be thought that older people could not adjust to overseas mission service. I was turned down at thirty because of age. Now there are thousands of retired people living in Mexico and elsewhere, not only adjusting well, but comfortably. All over the world expatriates of all ages are living in the interests of government and commerce. Why should religion be any different?

Missionary needs have undergone great changes recently. With the rise of modern nationalism, the new nations are reluctant to give visas to foreigners whose only purpose is the propagation of religion, but with open arms they welcome Christians who can teach, doctor, engineer, farm and carry on a trade. They badly need such people for the development of their countries, and this can be the most significant missionary service: living with the people and showing them the Christian way.

This was the New Testament pattern. The Apostle Paul labored as a tent maker in the cities he went to evangelize. The fact that he wasn't "full time" didn't seem to limit his success at all.

There are numerous opportunities at home, too. Retired people could volunteer their services to the churches as business managers, public relations directors, church visitors, building engineers, hostesses, secretaries and the like. This would free hard-pressed ministers for the spiritual work to which they were called, instead of having to spend time with the mechanics of church business. The Bible says (Acts 6:2): "It is not reason that we should leave the word of God and serve tables."

There is no real reason why a retired person could not become a minister for that matter. Most universities have a smattering of retired people studying for degrees that they have longed for all their lives, but couldn't get for financial reasons. To earn a B.D. degree is no more difficult than any other degree. What we need is people of any age, called by God, versed in the Scriptures, equipped to preach and minister to spiritual needs.

However, the vocational possibilities extend far beyond the religious callings. Every city has need for people to work for the common good. Many of these tasks have little or no money in them, but, as a rule, retired people don't require as much. At that age, they are usually aware that mere money-making is not particularly satisfying. Living and doing something worthwhile is far more rewarding.

It is surprising how many people go through life with a secret desire to be writers but never get around to it. Retirement provides a splendid opportunity to satisfy this need. True, many who attempt it will not make good, but they will have the fun of trying.

It should be mentioned that writing for publication is not easy. Most successful writers had to write hundreds of thousands of words before their product was chiseled into something saleable. It takes untold personal discipline and perseverance, but the need is there. The world is hungrier for the printed page than ever before. It is encouraging to note that an increasing number of older people seem to be breaking into the big time in this field.

After Grandma Moses, what is left to be said about art? If you have talent, it can be developed at any age. There is only one real way to find out — and that is try. You may not become famous, but you may find that creative art is one of the personality's greatest delicacies.

This is not intended to be a manual on retirement opportunities, but it is useless to talk in generalities. Here are specifics to prove that retirement is a transition to a new and exciting life and not the end of the road. Finding something exciting and absorbing to do will contribute more for health and long life than all the remedies in the world.

Since we tend to equate the body with the self rather than the building which houses the self, we are under a strong temptation to panic when the body begins to wear away. If we are not careful, the alarmed ego will clutch for pseudo-satisfaction in a number of unpleasant ways. The result may be so irritating to others that they may avoid us, which is even more disturbing to the personality ego. Let's examine some of these traps:

Self-pity is a common ailment of old age. It is a childish attempt of the unconscious mind to draw the attention of others to ourselves by our misfortunes. Once this process gets started, we have to continually outdo ourselves by producing more and larger troubles. Sometimes the mind will oblige by producing psychosomatic sickness for us, or we may become accident prone.

The development of this fault is insidious. Most victims of self-pity have no idea what has happened to them until they find that no one wants them any more. A good test is the kind of answer we give to the greeting: "How are you?" If we find ourselves eagerly recounting what is wrong with us, then we are in real trouble.

It is no use arguing that we are simply being honest. Everyone can find something wrong with himself, but each one of us also have a great deal more that is right! A healthy mind talks about the good and belittles the bad.

A critical spirit can make us as approachable as a porcupine. The psychology of this has been discussed earlier in this book. It is an attempt to make our egos look taller by pushing others down. It can become a compulsion in old age. The way to avoid it is to watch how we *think* about others, because, under this kind of pressure, the innermost thoughts will slip out into speech. There is no way to avoid the temptation to think derogatory things. It is what we do about such thoughts that counts. We can force the temptation to trigger a deliberate mental accounting of the good in the other person.

"Cold water treatment" of the ideas of others is not calculated to win friends and influence people. It is a panic reaction of the ego. When younger people come up with new ideas we tend to interpret them as rivals to our own, and so we proceed to massacre them. Actually, it is far more satisfying to the ego to treat new ideas gently, bringing out the best in them, and helping them on to fruition.

Demanding positions of authority or prestige is another ego disease of old age. The holding of office is a symbol of achievement so it is easy to see why we are reluctant to let it go. We may be deluded into believing that no one can do the job as well, or that everyone wants us to continue. Possibly this may even be true, but we will win greater respect by stepping aside gracefully and giving someone else an opportunity.

Some elderly people destroy the friendships they badly need by smothering them. After a while acquaintances shy away from making even the friendliest approach because they know they will be "nailed." It becomes almost impossible to get away from such people without being downright rude.

Children who love their aging parents dearly will tend to avoid them when this problem exists. Every person is a separate entity and will fight for his privacy and independence. There is a strong compulsion in age to bind our loved ones to us, because we are afraid of losing them. In reality the only way to preserve that love is to let them go.

There is a little larceny in all of us. What we cannot win, we are tempted to burglarize. The older person, feeling neglected by children busy with their own lives, may angrily or self-pityingly demand attention, respect, obedience. Of course, it never works. If we can't get the emotional response we need from others by just being ourselves, we won't gain it any other way. Personality burglary will lead us to the prison of our own isolation.

These ego ailments should not be treated in themselves alone. They are symptoms of a hungry personality. Whenever one such ailment occurs it is a signal to search for deeper satisfactions.

The person involved with the aged should understand what the basic problem is and needs. He is not aggravating because of sheer cussedness — he is desperately and blindly attempting to solve his inner problem. The best contribution you can make is to help him to ego fulfillments which will make his peculiarities unnecessary. It isn't easy, but this is the only remedy.

Lonesomeness is the endemic misery of old age. The older we get, the more we are left alone. Our friends and relatives pass on. Our children are busy with their own lives. At first the problem seems inevitable, but lonesomeness is not necessarily being physically alone. A person can be lonely in a crowded city and, on the other hand, the privacy of being alone can be a precious privilege. Lonesomeness is the emotion germinated by an unsatisfied personality, projected on to the circumstances of being alone.

There is much that we can do to cultivate friends, but we must take the initiative. When we complain that people are cold, unfriendly, unconcerned, we may be merely measuring their reaction to us. If we get busy contributing to the easing of their lonesomeness, we will be doing much to solve our own problem.

For every human being, the ultimate problem of living is death. Few people, even in advanced age, give much conscious thought to it — and this is as it should be. But the unconscious effect is great. The awareness of inevitable or impending cessa-

tion of earthly existence is unpleasant to the ego with its unending drive for a place in the sun.

The only answer is found in a strong religious faith. Faith
sees through the veil of flesh to the greater reality on the other
side. It recognizes that the true man is inside and that the
body is merely a temporary covering. Thus, if faith is strong
enough, the dissolution of the body is no more disturbing than
the throwing away of an old suit after it has worn out.

The Biblical picture of death is that of a transition: a meta-
morphosis. It is similar to the change in the caterpillar. When
its larval stage comes to an end, it looks as if its life is over.
All its movement is stilled and it hangs apparently dead, an
ugly blob on a twig of a tree. Then suddenly out of this decay
a butterfly emerges, ready and eager to start on a brand new
life. Now it is seen that the transition death was abundantly
worthwhile. The caterpillar life was limited to a slow crawl,
the butterfly life is infinitely richer and greater with a freedom
to move and fly, out of all comparison with the previous
existence.

This is a picture of death for the Christian: the transition to
an infinitely greater and more wonderful life in a medium free
from the limitations of earthly existence.

It takes a long time for the conviction of this truth to sink
deep enough into the unconscious mind to reassure the nervous
ego. In the long run, it depends largely on our awareness of
God. There is much more than intellectual assent to the existence of God — it must be experimental. We have to practice
God's presence continually and deliberately. Gradually the
truth breaks through and then we know.

Once we are aware of this spiritual union with God, un-
certainty about death vanishes. Being joined to Him, our
eternity becomes as certain as His.

I hope I have shown that the real weariness of old age is
mental and spiritual, and therefore curable. We will get tired,

but even in fatigue there is satisfaction and contentment, because life is sweet, significant and full of purpose. Then as the mountains of eternity begin to loom large on the horizon, instead of a sinking feeling, there will be a sense of thrill — an anticipation of a more significant life than ever before.